Getting started
in *Java*

In Preparation
by
Owen Bishop

BP561 Getting Started with *Java* Applets

Getting started in *Java*

by

Owen Bishop

**BERNARD BABANI (publishing) LTD
THE GRAMPIANS
SHEPHERDS BUSH ROAD
LONDON W6 7N
ENGLAND**

www.babanibooks.com

Please Note

Although every care has been taken with the production of this book to ensure that any projects, designs, listings, etc., contained herewith, operate in a correct and safe manner and also that any downloads specified are freely available on the World Wide Web, the Publisher and Author do not accept responsibility in any way for the failure (including fault in design) of any projects, designs, or listings to work correctly or to cause damage to any equipment that may be used, or in respect of any other damage or injury that may be so caused, nor do the Publishers accept responsibility in any way for the failure to obtain specified downloads.

ISBN 0 85934 554 8

Cover Design by Gregor Arthur

Printed and Bound in Great Britain by Cox & Wyman Ltd, Reading.

About the author

Owen Bishop is well known as a contributor to popular computing and electronics magazines and is the author of over 75 books, mostly in computing, electronics, and robotics. His talent for introducing technical subjects to beginners is proven by the many successful books he has written.

Acknowledgement

The *Limerick* program on pp. 62-4 is the *Java* version of a BBC BASIC program by Audrey and Owen Bishop (*Take Off with the Electron and BBC Micro*, Granada Publishing 1984).

Trademarks

Contents

1	Introducing *Java*	1
2	Setting up *Java*	5
3	Word programs	11
4	Working with numbers	23
5	Some input, some logic	33
Summing up Chapters 1 to 5		49
6	Arrays and other topics	55
7	A new look	71
8	OOP in action	81
9	Using constructors	93
10	Errors	105
Summing up Chapters 6 to 10		113
11	*Java* Packages	119
12	More about *swing*	127
13	Handy *swing* methods	143
14	Applets	155
15	*Graphics2D*	183
16	Finding the method	203
Postscript ...		211
Index		213

1 Introducing *Java*

The *Java* programming language was originated by Sun Microsystems in 1995. One of its more important features is that it is **portable**. For instance, a *Java* program written on a PC running *Windows 2000* will also run on computers running other versions of *Windows,* and on a Sun workstation, as well as on Unix, Linux and Apple computers. This book assumes that the reader is using *Windows*, the programs and displays having been created on a PC running *Windows XP*, but the programs should run equally well on the other platforms.

Java has achieved great popularity with programmers writing *Java* **applets** (short applications) for web pages, but it is also suitable for more extensive stand-alone applications. Both of these aspects of *Java* are illustrated in this book.

Another important and welcome feature of *Java* is that it is available as a **free** download from the Sun website. This book is based on the latest Version 1.5.0 of the Software Development Kit (SDK) popularly known as J2SE 5 (Java 2 Platform Standard Edition 5) or just *Java 2*, or *Tiger*. Chapter 2 outlines the procedure for downloading *Java* and setting it up on your computer.

Java has few keywords and relatively simple syntax. It is easy to learn and to use, once you have got used to the idea of **object-orientated programs** (see later). It is backed up by extensive libraries of program modules for performing particular tasks. These too can be downloaded free from Sun. They are readily incorporated into a user's programs, so saving time in project development. However, in spite of the fact that *Java* programming is quick and easy, the beginner is up against the initial hurdle of understanding the concepts of object orientated programming (or OOP, for short).The aim of this book is to help the reader get past this stage and confidently enter the world of OOP.

The approach of this book is to dive straight into writing short programs without bothering too much about their OOP features. Learning by doing and understanding by example is the way this book sets about getting you started in *Java*.

Object orientated programs

Although we propose to pick up the principles of OOP as we go along, there is something to be said for having just an outline idea of its main features. Perhaps the first question that might be asked is: 'What is an object?'. By 'object' we mean a relatively small, discrete, self-contained, block of program lines, performing a specific, and often single, function. In most other programming languages, the nearest equivalent to an object is a sub-routine, a function, or a procedure. *Java* differs in the way in which these objects are constructed, and the ways in which they can be linked together to create an application.

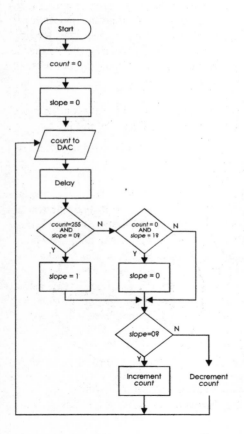

Fig. 1. A flowchart that defines the procedure for generating a sine waveform. The boxes of the chart show the steps in the procedure. The flowchart can be used as the basis for writing a program in a procedural language such as assembler or BASIC.

2

Most of the well-established programming languages are not object-orientated; they are **procedural.** These include the assemblers and the higher-level languages such as BASIC. A program in a procedural language is often represented by a flowchart (Fig.1). The flowchart has a series of process boxes (rectangles), which set out the procedure to be followed by the computer. There are stages in the flowchart for input and output and there are decision boxes where the path branches and the computer is directed along one branch or the other, depending on the result of a conditional test. There are usually jumps to subroutines to avoid the unnecessary repeat programming of frequently used routines.

In a procedural program, any one part of the program can interact with any other part, sharing data and definitions of variables. Unless great care is taken, such a program can become complex to analyse, leading to programming errors and unreliability. The complexity also makes it difficult, if not impossible, to amend sections of the program without undermining the programming of other sections.

In contrast, *Java* is object-orientated. An OOP is based on one or more relatively simple elements called **classes**, as illustrated in Fig. 2.

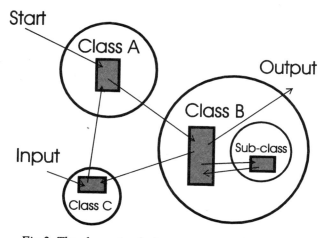

Fig 2. The elements of a Java *program. The shaded rectangles represent the data and methods of each class.*

3

The programmer defines a class by providing it with a set of **data** and with one or more **methods** for handling that data. The data and methods are **objects** which are to be handled in the way set out in the class. Methods are usually short program segments, and usually have procedural structure. In other words, they are short procedures, using many of the familiar programming devices such as input and output routines, 'for...while...' loops, and 'if...then...else' decision-taking. Readers who are used to writing procedural programs will still need these skills when writing *Java*.

The *Java* classes themselves are not objects, just as an engineer's blueprint of a bicycle is not a bicycle. Classes can be thought of as templates for building a program to perform a specfied task. Having defined a class we can construct an **instance** of the class, assigning it specific variables and parameters. A single class may thus result in many instances with differing properties, but similar functions.

With *Java,* each class and object is self-contained. A class accesses the data and methods of another class under strictly controlled conditions. This is called **encapsulation** and is described more fully on p. 117. It leads to reliability, robustness, economy of program space, and the ease with which an application can be contructed from new special-purpose classes and existing classes drawn from the class libraries. It simplifies maintenance as the program ages.

This leads us to consider the advantages of *Java* from the viewpoint of program development and maintainance. A newly written class is programmed and tested in isolation. After that, it can then be fitted in to the whole application with the confidence that it will work. Moreover, if it becomes necessary to amend or replace it, this can be done without upsetting the operation of other classes.

There is much more to be said about classes and the way they are linked, but this is deferred until we can look at some practical examples in Chapter 3 and beyond. In order to look at these, we need to install the software, as described in Chapter 2.

2 Setting up *Java*

The most usual way of obtaining the software is to visit the Sun website on the Internet. Its URL is:

http://java.sun.com

This site carries a wealth of information about *Java*, and the latest developments and updates. From here you can download the latest version of *Java*, suited to your computer. Follow the instructions on the screen. The download usually consists of a single executable file, about 90 MB in length. When unzipped, this produces a number of folders each containing numerous files.

In PCs, *Java* is run from a command line, that is, in the same way as running a DOS program. If your computer is running *Windows 95, 98, NT* or *2000*, click on the MS-DOS icon to obtain the DOS screen. In *Windows XP*, get the command line by first clicking on the 'Start' button at the bottom left of the screen. Then click 'Run'. When the small 'Run' window appears, type 'cmd' (without the quotes) and click on OK.

In the DOS or command line window, the lowest line contains text beginning with 'C:\'. This indicates that you are working in the root directory of the computer, on Drive C. You may find that there is other text following the 'C:\', such as the name of one of the folders saved on your hard disc. The names are separated by backslashes. In Fig. 4 (overleaf), the line is:

C:\Documents and Settings\Owen

In this case we are working in the 'Owen' sub-directory of the 'Documents and Settings' sub-directory of the 'C:' directory. Note that a 'directory' is what *Windows* calls a 'folder'.

If so, you are at present working in a sub-directory and you need to get back to the root directory.

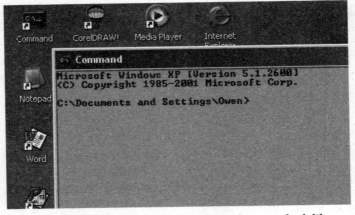

Fig. 3. The command line or DOS window may look like this when it is first called, or it may have other directories listed after the 'C:\'. Note: for clarity, the colours of the command window have been set to black on light grey (see p. 9).

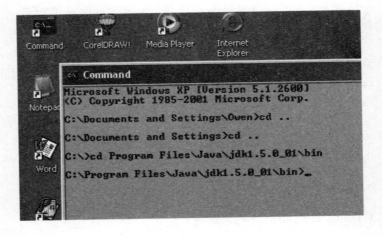

Fig. 4. This shows the stages of getting to the root directory and, from there, to the directory containing the main Java files.

The first step is to navigate back to the root directory. Do this by typing 'CD ..' and press Enter. The letters 'CD' mean 'change directory' and the two full-stops mean 'to the next higher directory'. Do not forget to leave a space after 'CD'. In our example we need to do this twice to get back to the root directory. Fig. 4 shows the sequence.

Fig. 4 also shows the stages in getting to the sub-directory in which the executable *Java* files are held. Once again we use 'CD' but this time followed by the sub-directory names, separated by backslashes (see p. 9) to get to a sub-directory within a subdirectory. In the example, we are running version 1.5.0 of *Java 2*, which is in the 'bin' subdirectory of the 'jdk1.5.0_01' subdirectory. This is in the 'Java' subdirectory of the Program Files directory. You should use the names of whatever subdirectories *Java* has installed itself. The screen is shown in Fig. 4 as it should be when the computer is waiting for further instructions, to compile or run a *Java* program.

Versions

Like most pieces of software, *Java* is continually being updated. At the time of writing, the current Version is 1.5.0. This is one of the options available from Sun Microsystems as a download. All the programs in this book will work with this version. If you already have an earlier version of *Java 2*, you can use this instead for most of the programs. You can upgrade to Version 1.5.0 later.

Java is also available from other sources. The more advanced books on programming in *Java* often include a CD-ROM that has the complete software on it. You can download from this instead of from the website. The only possible disadvantage is that this might be Java 1 which does not include all the graphics facilities that we use in this book.

Writing, compiling and running

We shall give fuller details on these topics in the next chapter, but this outline introduces the main stages in creating and testing progams. This is a three-stage process.

The first stage is to **write** the program, using simple text editing software, such as *WordPad* or *Notepad*. If you have a PC running *Windows* software, one or both of these programs are provided with it. *Notepad* saves text as simple text files, with no embedded formatting. The file name has the '.txt' extension. But *WordPad* can also save text in other formats, such as Rich Text Format. This includes non-printing codes for formatting the text. If you save your program text in one of these other formats, you will receive dozens of error messages as *Java* tries to make sense of the codes in the file. When you save the file always select 'Text Document' in the 'Save as type:' box at the bottom of the 'Save as...' window.

When you have written part or the whole of a program and, after you have inspected it for obvious errors, you use a program called *javac* to compile it (see p. 15) This turns your text into a coded version that *Java* can understand. This is known as **bytecode**. It is a half-way stage between your text file and the final runnable version of the program.

While it is compiling your text, *javac* is busily scanning it for errors. As it finds these, it prints a list of them on the screen. These are known as **compile-time errors**. You may feel daunted, especially when you are first starting, when a long list of errors appears. Quite often things are not as bad as they seem. What happens is that a very small error, such as a missing bracket you forgot to type, so confuses the compiler that it loses track of the program, and it subsequently 'finds errors' that are not really there. If you look through your text and insert the missing bracket, half-a-dozen or more reported errors will have miraculously 'disappeared' when you re-compile the program.

Compiling produces a file with the same filename as your original text, but with the extension '.class'. Use the *java* program to run this (see p. 16). The program may run perfectly at this stage but occasionally there is something in the structure of the program that produces one or more **run-time errors**. You should not expect to have many of these. The *java* program reports these on the screen and stops running.

To correct run-time errors, you need to return to the original text to locate and correct the errors, then re-compile the text using *javac*. Finally, run *java* to interpret the newly-compiled '.class' file.

Backslash

If your keyboard is set to English (United Kingdom), you may find that you get a hash (#) when you press the backslash (\) key. To get a backslash, press *and hold* the Alternate (ALT) key *and* the F1 key while you type 092 on the *numeric keypad*. Release the ALT and F1 keys and a backslash will appear. Note that this does not work if you key 092 using the number keys above the QWERTY keys.

Display colours

By default, the command line window displays light grey text on a black background. You may be satisfied with this — in some ways it makes you feel 'near to' your computer's operations. But you can have other colours if you prefer.

The exact technique for altering the colours depends on the computer. For *Windows XP*, display the command line window as previously instructed. Then move the cursor to the title bar at the top of the command window and click *right*. From the drop-down menu, select 'Defaults', which displays a window titled 'Console Windows Properties'. Click on the 'Screen text' button, then on one of the colours displayed below it. Click on the 'Screen background', then select a contrasting colour from the display. A small window shows the 'Selected screen colors', so you can see the effect. For writing this book we chose yellow text on a blue background, which gives a cheerful and legible display. For the screen shots we chose black text on a light grey background. You can try out various combinations before clicking on the 'OK' button to activate your choice. Of course, you can always come back again later and select new colours.

3 Word programs

In this chapter we look at and run two short programs, using them to illustrate some of the more important terms and keywords. Read through the chapter first. Then boot up your computer and follow through the sequence from writing the text to running the compiled version, using *java*.

The first step is to run your text editor program. Type in the text, exactly as in Fig. 5. We used *Notepad* and the font is `Courier New`. We use the same font in the text of this book when we are quoting programs or extracts from programs.

```
/* This is a multi-line comment.
It is ignored by the Java compiler. */

public class FirstProgram {
        public static void main(string[] args) {
        // This is a one-line comment, also ignored.
                System.out.println("Your first Java program");
        }
}
```

Fig. 5. FirstProgram, *as it appears in* Notepad.

So that you do not have to turn the page as you read the explanations, the program is printed again overleaf.

The first thing to notice is that there are two **comments** in it. These provide information about the program; for instance, its name, what it does, or how it works. Comments are very helpful to a person studying the program, but are ignored by the *javac* compiler.

Many people do not use the multi-line comment format. They type long comments on consecutive lines as single-line comments, each beginning with //.

Here is *FirstProgram* again:

```
        /* This is a multi-line comment.
        It is ignored by the javac compiler */
public class FirstProgram {
        public static void main(String[] args) {
        // This is a one-line comment, also ignored  .
        System.out.println("Your first Java program");
        }
}
```

We can see the form of the program more easily if we leave out the two comments:

```
public class FirstProgram {
        public static void main(String[] args) {

        System.out.println("Your first Java program");
        }
}
```

As you will discover when you run this program, it prints a message on the screen: "Your first Java program". The line that does this is:

```
System.out.println("Your first Java program");
```

This example demonstrates how the actual program (or the **method**, as it is called) is encapsulated (p. 4) in a protective and isolating 'wall' of curly brackets and definition statements.

Now to examine the outer layers! The first line states in effect that the text following it, and enclosed in curly brackets, defines a **class**, called *FirstProgram*. We can call it anything we like, provided that we do not use words that are reserved as keywords. It is also a good idea not to use the names of existing classes. For this reason, it is best to use a name that describes fairly closely what the class is or what it does.

The keyword `public` is easy to understand. It means that this class is accessible by other objects in the package. In most of our examples a class definition begins with this word. The statement on the first line ends with an opening curly bracket. This and its corresponding closing curly bracket on the last line enclose the body of the class.

The second line of the program indicates that the text following it defines a **method**, something that the class *does*. We see that this is a `public` method (open to all). It is also a `static` method, which means that it is always active, it does not 'come and go'. The word `void` means that it does not return any values to any routine that calls it. Most method definitions in this book have the same features so they are all defined in the same way, using the keywords `public static void`. If you do not fully understand what they mean, or what difference it makes when alternative words are used, it does not matter at this stage. Their actions here and when to use other keywords instead of them will become clearer with experience.

The last word in the method header is main, the category of the method. Every program must have a `main` method, for this is the one with which the program begins when it is run. In this example it is the only method. Following its category, a method usually has a list of one or more **parameters** enclosed in round brackets. These are values being passed to the method from outside it. Note that, because a method is always defined with a set of one or more parameters (objects to work on) it is usual to add these brackets when referring to the method. Thus, we refer to the main method as `main()`. This helps readers to know if a given object is a method or not.

In this example, the parameter in the brackets is a string variable (p. 17) in the form of an array of strings (called arguments) that are keyed in on the command line before the program is run. Later, we will use this technique for supplying data to a program. However, although this technique is very useful for short programs intended for demonstrating programming in *Java,* there are several much more visually effective and preferred ways of supplying data. So, input from the command line is not often used, except for the introductory examples in beginners' books, but we still need to list the parameters of the `main` method as `(String[] args)`.

Note that `args` is short for `arguments` and *java* understands both forms.

The third line defines the method. Someone has already written a program that takes a string array and prints it out on the computer screen. There is no need for you to repeat all that complicated programming — just call the method. The method we are using here is called `println()`. To locate it, and to refer the computer to the operations required to perform it, you simply refer to the class (`System`) and object (`out`) in which its definition is to be found. This book provides many such references to useful methods, and you will soon get to know the most commonly used ones. Also, there are books that provide complete lists (with descriptions) of all existing methods. When you refer to a method in this way, you do not need to know how it works. But you can rely on it doing its job properly because it has been well tested by experts. And it works on any of the main computer platforms. The method is called by keying in the three names in order, separated by dots:

```
System.out.println()
```

Being a method, `println()` is followed by round brackets containing parameters. `println()` expects a string, either declared at the time by typing it out in full between double quotes (as here), or by naming a string variable that has been declared previously. When the program is run it calls up the method filed elsewhere in the same directory. This takes the string of text and prints it on the screen. Calling ready-written methods is an important feature of *Java*. When you download *Java* from the Sun website, you get more than just the *Java* programs. You also get extensive libraries of classes and methods that are there, waiting to be used in your own programs. Familiarising yourself with the contents of these libraries is an essential aspect of becoming proficient at *Java* programming.

Note that the program line ends with a semicolon (;). All lines that tell the computer to DO something must end with this. There is only one line in this program that leads to any activity by the computer so this is the only line ending in a semicolon. The statement ends with a closing curly bracket on the 4th line.

14

In this program, the text fits on a single line on the screen. Sometimes you may have longer text that extends over two or more lines *on the screen*. Running on from one line to the next is allowed, provided that there is only one semicolon, placed after the final *screen* line. The many lines of text count as only one *program* line.

Compiling

When you have typed in the program *and checked it through,* save it as a *text file* with extension '.java', in your working directory. Note: do NOT save it with the '.txt' extension. The file *must* be saved under exactly the same name as the class it defines, but with the extension '.java'. The class name of this program is *FirstProgram*, so save it as 'FirstProgram.java.' *Java* is case-sensitive, so this program must *not* be saved as 'Firstprogram.java', or 'firstprogram.java', or other versions in which the cases do not match exactly.

Fig. 6. The command window ready to invoke javac *to compile* FirstProgram. *Note that the confusing screen text associated with navigating to the* bin *sub-directory has been removed by typing CLS (= clear screen) and pressing Enter.*

Then we keyed in 'javac FirstProgram.java'. The program name is one word.

15

Now press 'Enter'. The flashing underline cursor after the word 'java' moves to the start of the next line. There is a pause of several seconds while the program is compiled. Then the prompt appears on the left.

It is at this stage that compile-time errors, if any, are reported. If there are errors, you need to deal with them now. Errors that are easy to make include:

1) Missing semicolon at the end of each programming line.
2) Missing curly bracket, or bracket facing the wrong way.
3) Using single quotes (') instead of double quotes (").
4) Case errors, for example, typing 'Firstprogram' instead of 'FirstProgram'.
5) Not indicating comments by /* and */, or by //.

Assuming that errors have been corrected, run the program by typing `java FirstProgram` and pressing 'Enter'. After a delay of several seconds, the programmed message appears on the screen:

```
Your first Java program
```

Fig. 7. The screen after running FirstProgram. *On the lowest line, the command prompt awaits your next instructions.*

More ways with strings

Java has several ways of handling strings. One of these is a class called *StringTokenizer*. This is able to chop strings of characters into shorter strings, called **tokens**. To find out some of the things it can do, run your text editor and key in the program shown in Fig. 8.

```
import java.util.StringTokenizer;

class FlightLegs {

        public static void main(String[] args) {

        StringTokenizer st1;

        String route = "Heathrow-Zurich-Singapore-Perth";
        st1 = new StringTokenizer(route, "-");

        System.out.println("Departure from: " + st1.nextToken())
        System.out.println("Calling at: " + st1.nextToken());
        System.out.println("And: " + st1.nextToken());
        System.out.println("Destination: " + st1.nextToken());
        }
```

Fig. 8. The FlightLegs *program as it appears in* Notepad.

StringTokenizer is not normally used when *java* is running a program. It has to be obtained from the library of classes and methods that is included in the *java* software. This is why this program begins with an instruction to import *StringTokenizer*. The first line shows that it is to be found in a package of classes called *util* (short for utilities), which is to be found in a larger package called *java*. Having done this, we do not need to type java.util.StringTokenizer every time we want to refer to the class.

17

To save page-turning, here is *FlightLegs* again:

```
import java.util.StringTokenizer;

class FlightLegs {

        public static void main(String[] args) {

        StringTokenizer st1;

        String route = "Heathrow-Zurich-Singapore-Perth";
        st1 = new StringTokenizer(route, "-");

        System.out.println("Departure from: " +
st1.nextToken());
        System.out.println("Calling at: " +
st1.nextToken());
        System.out.println("And: " + st1.nextToken());
        System.out.println("Destination: " +
st1.nextToken());
        }
}
```

After importing the class, the program goes on to define a class called *FlightLegs* (so we must save this program as 'FlightLegs.java'). The main method is defined by the usual formula: public static and so on. The first program statement (remember, it must end with a semi-colon) is:

StringTokenizer st1;

This is creating a *StringTokenizer* object and naming it st1. This kind of operation is unfamiliar to some people but it becomes plainer if we compare it with creating a number variable. In *Java*, if we want to create a variable to, say, hold the number of members of a club, we write this:

int members;

The int means an integer variable, that is, a whole number with no fractions. We need an integer variable (there are other kinds, see p. 49) because there are no fractions of members in a club. This particular integer variable is called members for obvious reasons. Members can later be given a value. Similarly, we create a *StringTok-enizer* object, called st1 and give it a value later.

The next statement creates another object, a *String* variable called `route`. Here we go on straight away to give it a value, which is the string of airport names. This is enclosed in double quotes. Note that the names are separated by hyphens.

Now we give `st1` a value, that of a new object of the *StringTokenizer* class. We use one of the methods of this class. The method has two parameters passed to it. One is the name of the string that it is to tokenize. The second parameter is the character that separates the tokens. Here the parameters are `route` and a hyphen, the latter indicated by the hyphen character in double quotes. More than one token separator can be listed. If no separator is listed the routine splits the string at a space, a tab, a new line, and a carriage return.

Now we are ready to begin splitting up the string! The tokens are printed on the screen using that `println()` method that we used for *FirstProgram*. The parameter of each `println()` statement consists of text, in double quotes, a plus symbol, and the expression `st1.nextToken()`. The plus symbol means that the text string and the token are to be **concatenated**. That is, they are to be joined together to make a single string and printed out as such. The `nextToken()` method is one of the methods of *StringTokenizer*. Its job is to select the tokens in order from the split string. The method is told which string to split by prefixing the expression with its name, `st1`.

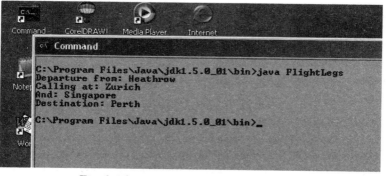

Fig. 9. The result of running FlightLegs.

19

Program format - a summary

These two example programs illustrate a simple, though typical, way of creating a class in *Java*. There are many other additions and variations that we will describe in later chapters, but these programs cover some of the essentials.

Summing up, a program consists of:

An `import` statement, if needed, to call up the less frequently used classes and their methods.

```
class name {

    public static void main (String[] args) {

        data: declarations of class variables and objects and the
        values of some or all of these;

        methods: program lines to work on these;

    }
}
```

Things to do

Familiarise yourself with the writing-compiling-running routine by writing modified versions of *FirstProgram* and *FlightLegs*. For example, write a program called *SecondProgram* that displays a different message. Do not repeat the comments from *FirstProgram*, but add some of your own. Include comments that help to remind *you* about the program structure and what the program does.

You could try using *StringTokenizer* (remember that it is spelt with a 'z', not an 's'). For example, take a message such as "This is really good fun"and display it as separate words. Another task is to take a date such as 21/9/05 and split it into day, month and year. In the printout routine, try to put '20' in front of the year so that it reads '2005'.

You may like to include some **character escape codes** in the text of your program. These control the displaying of the text. Useful codes include:

\n which causes the computer to start a new line,
\t which causes the computer to 'tab', and
\f which causes a formfeed.

Just include the code in the text; it will not print out but will simply cause the action described. For example:

           "Yew Tree House,\nWiseton,\nNotts."

Prints as:

Yew Tree House,
Wiseton,
Notts.

If the text includes single or double quotes, this can lead to confusion. Helpfully, there are escape codes for these:

\' which prints a single quote
\" which prints a double quote

Try using these codes in your text.

4 Working with numbers

The program below is given two numbers, divides one by the other and reports on the result of the calculation. It is a simple program but gives us the chance to look again at some of the concepts of *Java* and to study some new ones. Here is the program, called *Divide*:

```
class Divide {
        int     dividend;
        int     divisor;
        int     result;
        int     remainder;

        void calculate() {
                result = dividend / divisor;
                remainder = dividend % divisor;
        }

        void Printout() {
                System.out.println("Result = " + result);
                System.out.println("Remainder = " +
remainder);
        }

public static void main(String[] args) {

        Divide Divide1 = new Divide();
        Divide1.dividend = 35;
        Divide1.divisor = 4;
        Divide1.calculate();
        System.out.println("The first division yields:");
        Divide1.Printout();

        Divide Divide2 = new Divide();
        Divide2.dividend = 99;
        Divide2.divisor = 31;
        Divide2.calculate();
        System.out.println("The second division yields:");
        Divide2.Printout();
        }       }
```

It is obvious that this program has more parts to it than the two programs of Chapter 3. Like *FirstProgram*, it begins with a statement that it is defining a class, which on this occasion is called *Divide*. From then on, we come to some new ideas.

The first stage is to define some variables for the class method to use. The keyword `int` indicates that the four variables are defined as **integer** variables. An integer is a 'natural' or 'counting' number, or we describe it as a 'whole number', without any fractions appended to it. Integers may be positive or negative and include the number '0'. In *Java*, integers are limited to the range −2 147 483 648 to +2 147 483 647, which is large enough for almost all purposes. The advantage of using integers rather than other types of number (see later) is that they are processed faster.

The variables are given **identifiers** (names). As usual, we can choose any name we like, provided that it is not a reserved keyword. It makes it easier to follow the program if we choose identifiers that indicate the function of each variable in the maths that is to follow. Note again that each line ends in a semicolon. It is permissible to define all the integers on one line. The four definitions could be replaced by a list of the identifiers:

```
int   dividend, divisor, result, remainder;
```

These variables are examples of **instance variables**. They are variables that can be used, perhaps with different values, to describe different **instances** of the *Divide* class. Different instances of the class are different examples of division, such as 4/7, 34/2, 144/39, ... and so on.

Because they are instance variables, these variables do not exist outside of the curly brackets in which they are defined. We could use the same names within another set of curly brackets and there would be no confusion (to the computer, at least, though the programmer might be bewildered!). This is another illustration of encapsulation in *Java*.

Having defined the variables, we now have to define what is to be done with them. In this example, we define two **instance methods**. One, called `calculate()`, is to perform the division. The other, called `Printout()`, is to display the outcome of the calculation on the screen in a prescribed format. These instance methods differ from the `main` method in that they do not begin with `public static`.

24

The `calculate()` method performs two calculations. The first is a simple division: `dividend / divisor`. The division operator is the conventional 'slash' symbol, but note that there must be a space on either side of it. In *Java*, dividing one integer by another always yields an integer as the `result`. For example, dividing 37 by 5 gives 7. The remainder is ignored.

If we need the remainder, as we do here, we must calculate it separately. So the `calculate` method also includes a line that calculates the `remainder`. This uses the **modulo** operator (%). For example 37 % 5 gives 2.

The second instance method is called `Printout()`. It displays the outcome of the calculations. We have decided on a two-line display. As on p. 11, we use `System.out.println()`. In the brackets we type a short text string (in quotes), followed by a plus symbol to join the string to a printout of the value of the variable (NOT in quotes).

The two methods complete the definition of the *Divide* class. It is a template for performing a division and displaying the results. Try to think of a class as a template for 'doing something'. It tells the computer what variables to use and what to do with them. It *may* tell the computer the values of the variables but, being a template, it does not necessarily have to do this. Note that the blocks of code for the two methods are each enclosed in curly brackets.

Instances of the *Divide* class

Having set up variables and methods for use by the class, we are now ready to create some special instances of the class. The main method takes care of this. It is introduced by the same line with the same structure as was used on p. 11:

```
public static void main(String[] args)
```

The keyword `main` shows that this is where the action begins! There are to be two instances of division, 35/4 and 99/31. Before we look at these in detail, consider the simpler case in which we want to perform only the first division, 35/4. We could do it like this:

```
dividend = 35;
divisor = 4;
calculate()      //Calls the first method, to
                 //calculate result and remainder.
Printout()       //Calls the second method to
                 //display result and remainder.
```

This program segment shows the basic structure of the `main` method. It calls on the two previously defined class methods. We have only to type `calculate()` and the computer is sent back to look up the definition of `calculate()`, and then uses the declared values of `dividend` and `divisor`. From these, it calculates `result` and `remainder` and goes back to `Printout()` to discover how to display them.

However, *Divide* is more complicated than the short program above. It performs two different divisions using two different sets of values of the variables. This is why the main method of *Divide* contains two *instances* of the class, one for dividing 35 by 4 and the other for dividing 99 by 31. The instances are identical except for the values assigned to the variables. Each calculates values for `result` and `remainder`, and then displays them.

The variables may have different values in the two instances but they are both part of the main method, inside the *same* pair of curly brackets. We can not allow them to have the same names. To prevent the computer becoming confused, we preface the variable name with an instance name. We begin by creating a new instance of the *Divide* class, called *Divide1*:

```
Divide Divide1 = new Divide();
```

We have chosen *Divide1* as the instance name but, as long as we conform to the usual restrictions on naming (p. 11), we can call it anything we like. This instance is a replica of the original class, in which the components of the class are identified by prefacing the names with 'Divide1'. For example, the instance has its own set of variables, such as `Divide1.dividend`, and its own set of methods, `Divide1.calculate()` and `Divide1.Printout()`.

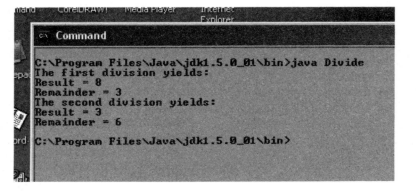

Fig. 10. The result of running the Divide *program.*

Programming equations

Many people who study physics at school will be familiar with the so-called **equations of motion.** This program uses two of them to calculate the final speed and distance travelled by two cars, given their initial speed, their acceleration (assumed to be constant) and the elapsed time.

Here is the program:

```
class motion {

        //This class is based on the equations of
        //uniformly accelerated linear motion.

        double initialSpeed;    //metres per second.
        double finalSpeed;      //metres per second.
        double accel;   //metres per second per second.
        double time;    //seconds.
        double distance;        //metres.
        String model;
```

27

```
        void workItOut() {
                finalSpeed = initialSpeed + accel * time;
                distance = (initialSpeed + finalSpeed) / 2
* time;
        }

        void Printout() {
                System.out.println("The " + model + "
reaches " + finalSpeed + " m/s\nat " + distance + " m from
the start.");
        }

public static void main(String[] args) {

        motion OldBanger = new motion();
        OldBanger.initialSpeed = 9;
        OldBanger.accel = 0.5;
        OldBanger.time = 10;
        OldBanger.model = "old banger";
        OldBanger.workItOut();
        OldBanger.Printout();

        motion SoupedUp = new motion();
        SoupedUp.initialSpeed = 0;
        SoupedUp.accel = 45;
        SoupedUp.time = 10;
        SoupedUp.model = "souped up car";
        SoupedUp.workItOut();
        SoupedUp.Printout();
        }
}
```

The program has the same general structure as *Divide,* but there are some interesting points to consider. In begins with declarations of the variables to be used; the comments indicate the units in which the variables are to be expressed. In this program we have used double-precision floating point variables. This allows us to work with decimals for any of the quantities. The float type of floating point variables has lower precision that is still more that adequate for the calculations in this progam. However, *Java* sometimes automatically converts float to double, which may lead to complications. It is safer to use double from the start.

This program also defines a name for the vehicle described by each instance, so we declare a string variable to hold this. Note that this variable type has an initial capital letter, String.

The program has two method definitions. The first is called work-ItOut(). It might have been called calculate(), as in the previous program, for it does a similar job. Given the initial speed, the acceleration and the elapsed time, it calculates the final velocity. Then, using the calculated value of the final velocity, the initial speed and the elapsed time, it calculates the distance travelled.

The two equations in *workItOut* illustrate some points about setting out equations. The first equation contains two **arithmetical operators**, + (add) and * (multiply). It is important that the computer performs these operations in the correct order. In some systems, the computer operates from left to right. If the initial speed is 9 m/s, the acceleration is 0.5 m/s/s and the time is 10 s, the result would be:

final speed = 9 + 0.5 * 10 = 9.5 * 10 = 95 m/s.

This is clearly wrong. In *Java*, as in many other languages, there is a definite order of **precedence** for evaluating complex expressions. In most languages, including *Java*, multiplication and division take precedence over addition and subtraction. In our sample expression, the multiplication is effected before the addition, so the result is:

final speed = 9 + 0.5 * 10 = 9 + 5 = 14 m/s

This is the correct answer. In the second equation the operators are +, / and *. But we do not want the computer to divide final speed by 2, which would happen if division takes precedence over addition. To avoid this, we place the addition inside brackets. Brackets take precedence over all other operators, and the contents of brackets are evaluated first, *then* division or multiplication:

distance = (9 + 15)/2 * 10 = 24/2 *10 = 120

The second method in this class is Printout(), which is the same as we used in *Divide*, but with different parameters. Note the use of the character escape code, \n. This tells the computer where to break the line and start a new one. It does not have spaces on either side of it.

In the `main` method we create two instances of *motion*, called *OldBanger* and *SoupedUp*, to represent two types of automobile. These initialise `initialSpeed`, `accel`, and `time` with particular values for each instance of the cars and then calculate the resulting `finalSpeed` and `distance`. We also initialise the `model` string variable with a text phrase that describes the type of car. When the results are printed out , we shall know to which cars the figures refer.

As in *Divide*, the two instances have exactly the same format. Each type of car has its own set of variables, with their own set of values, all identified by the prefix `OldBanger` or `SoupedUp`. After evaluation, the corresponding sets of results are called up and displayed using the same instance names.

In both of the programs in this chapter we have treated the two instances as separate entities. However, we can mix their values in the same program line. The computer will go to each instance to obtain the required data. For example, assume the two vehicles start from the same point. The souped-up car is standing still, waiting to go. The old banger comes up from behind and is running at 9 m/s as it reaches the souped up car. The latter accelerates away at that instant. What is the distance between them after 10 s? The calculation is simple:

```
lagBehind = SoupedUp.distance - OldBanger.distance;
        System.out.println("The " + OldBanger.model + " is
" + lagBehind + " m behind the " + SoupedUp.model);
```

You could insert these two lines just before the pair of closing backets in the listing. See how we are mixing data from the *SoupedUp* and *OldBanger* instances, both in the calculations and in the printing statement.

Before this line can be used we need to declare the double variable `lagBehind`. There is a slight complication here. The variables declared at the beginning of the class definition are **class variables**. When a class instance is created, it is given its own copies of the class variables. For example, `OldBanger.time` is the copy of the `time` variable given to the *OldBanger* instance.

The class *SoupedUp* has another copy of this variable, called `SoupedUp.time`. These copies can be given values and have them changed independently. But `lagBehind` is different. It has not been copied to the instances. Its name does not include an instance name. It is a class variable, which holds the same value whether it is used by *OldBanger* or by *SoupedUp*. To prevent it being changed by either of the instances, it must be made `static`. This can be done when the variable is declared, like this:

```
static double lagBehind;          //metres.
```

Type this at the end of the variable list at the beginning of the program. Then compile the program, using *javac* and run it, using *java*.

Things to do

1 You now have the framework of a calculator class that can be adapted to perform other calculations (perhaps with more than two variables), and other display formats. Try adapting the program for other calculating routines, using these mathematical operators:

Mathematical Operators	
+	addition
−	subtraction
*	multiplication
/	division
%	modulus

2 Investigate the precedence of the operators. For example, note the difference between 4 * 5 + 6 and 4 + 5 * 6. Note the action of the brackets. For example, note the difference between 4 * 5 + 6 and 4 * (5 + 6).

3 Use number types other than integers. Define floating-point numbers as `float` (range 1.4e-045 to 3.4e038). Sometimes the compiler will suggest that the number be defined as double (range 4.9e-324 to 1.7e308). You type in floating-point numbers using a full-stop as the decimal point, or you can use the exponential notation.

5 Some input, some logic

The programs we have studied in earlier chapters have all taken the values of the variables from statements within the program. Now we look at a simple technique which supplies a program with data that has been typed on the command line. The program below calculates the surface area and the volume of a rectangular prism, given its length, width and height (or depth).

```
class RectangularPrism {

    public static void main(String[] args) {

    int length = 0;
    int width = 0;
    int height = 0;
    int area = 0;
    int volume = 0;

    if (args.length > 0)
        length = Integer.parseInt(args[0]);
    if (args.length > 1)
        width = Integer.parseInt(args[1]);
    if (args.length > 2)
        height = Integer.parseInt(args[2]);

    area = 2 * (length * width + length * height +
width * height);
    volume = length * width * height;

    System.out.println("\nArea = " + area + "\nVolume
= " + volume);
    }
}
```

The program is run by the command `java RectangularPrism`, followed by three integers, separated by spaces, that are the dimensions of the prism. For example, the command might be:

```
java RectangularPrism 5 42 18
```

As usual, the first step in the program is to declare the variables. Here we have three, for the three dimensions of the prism. The other two are for the results of the calculations. All the variables are initialised with the value '0' at the same time as they are declared.

Variables may be initialised when declared, as in this program, or simply declared with no given value, as on p. 27. Here they are given a value just in case the reader fails to key in three values and this leads to complications later.

The next stage is to read in the values that have been typed in as arguments on the command line (abbreviated as `args` in the listing). Although they appear to be integers, they are automatically read into a special array in the form of strings. As we shall see later, it is also possible to input string variables on the command line. The program proceeds to check through the arguments to allocate them to the integer variables `dim1`, `dim2` and `dim3`.

This part of the program illustrates the use of the familiar logical structure, if ... then (except that the keyword 'then' is omitted):

```
if    (args.length > 0)
```

The expression in brackets states a condition, that is either true or false. In other words, the expression has a **Boolean** value. It calls on a method (called `length`) of the `arguments` class. This method looks at the arguments (if any) on the command line and counts them. In this case the value returned by `args.length` is 3. Because 3 *is* greater than 0, the expression in brackets is evaluated as `true`. So the program goes on to the next line, which calls up a method (called `parseInt`) of the `Integer` class.

These two examples of calling methods, `args.length` and `Integer.parseInt`, illustrate how *Java* works as a set of classes, each calling on elements belonging to the others. They also show how programming in *Java* is made easy by the class libraries. There is no need for us to 're-invent the wheel' in order to read from the command line. All we need to know is the name of a method within a class that will do the job for us. We do not need to know the details of the program of the class and method, but we need to know what parameters (if any) must be passed to the method when we call it. No parameter is needed for `args.length`. `Integer.parseInt` needs to be told the position in the `arguments` array of the string that it is to work on. Here, the positions run from 0 to 2.

The routine for reading the command line and converting the strings into integer variables is designed not to crash should the user not type in enough dimensions. Having found that there is at least one dimension on the line, this (args [0]) is assigned to dim1. Then, having found that there are at least two dimensions, the next (args[1]) is assigned to dim2. Finally, having found that there are at least three dimensions, the third one (args[2]) is assigned to dim3. Any further dimensions, entered by mistake, are ignored.

The next stage in the program calculates area and volume. Note the bracketing in the expression for area. It ensures that the areas are summed before their sum is multiplied by 2. The printout makes use of \n twice: (1) to provide a blank line between the command line and the display, and (2) to put the area and volume on separate lines. Fig. 11 shows the result of a typical run of this program.

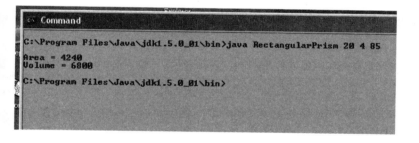

Fig. 11. The RectangularPrism *program calculates surface area and volume, given three dimensions in the command line.*

Temperature converter

Here is a program that you could usefully retain on your computer. Given a temperature in degrees Celsius, it converts it to Fahrenheit. Given a temperature in degrees Fahrenheit, it converts it to Celsius.

The program has many features in common with the previous one. It begins by declaring two input and two output variables. In this case the variables are integers and strings. The listing is:

```
class ConvertTemp {

        public static void main(String[] args) {

                int temp = 0;
                String scale = "You need temperature and
scale.";
                String cel = "Celsius";
                String fah = "Fahrenheit";

                if (args.length > 0)
                        temp = Integer.parseInt(args[0]);
                if (args.length > 1)
                        scale = args[1];

                if (scale.equals(cel)){
                        temp = temp * 9 / 5 + 32;
                        scale = fah;
                }

                else if (scale.equals(fah)){
                        temp = (temp - 32) * 5 / 9;
                        scale = cel;
                }


                System.out.println("\nTemperature is " +
temp + " " + scale);

        }
}
```

In the original listing for this program the array name arguments was spelt out in full, five times. To save a lot of typing (and possible errors), *Java* allows us to shorten arguments to args. Shortening this frequently-used name makes program lines shorter and therefore easier to set out clearly. But you must be consistent and use the short form throughout the program.

The string scale eventually holds the name of the temperature scale, but is initialised with an error message, in case the user does not key in sufficient arguments. The correct input (on the command line) is a number and a word (Celsius or Fahrenheit).

Reading the temperature and scale into the variables `temp` and `scale` follows a routine similar to that of the previous program. Because `scale` is a string variable, it can be read straight from the `argument array`, without using `Integer.parseInt()`.

Then follow two logic blocks. The first tests `scale`, to find out if it has the value `Celsius`. If so, `temp` is converted to its Fahrenheit equivalent and `scale` is given the value `Fahrenheit`. If this test fails, the program uses the `else if...` construction to employ an alternative test. If successful, this converts Fahrenheit to Celsius. If both tests fail, `temp` and `scale` retain their original default values, 0 and "`You need temperature and scale.`".

Finally, the results of the calculation are displayed on the screen. Fig. 12 shows two typical runs of this program.

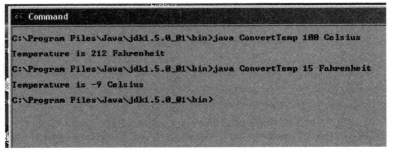

Fig. 12. The ConvertTemp *program automatically performs conversions in the required direction.*

This program uses integer variables and involves division. Any fraction in the result is simply chopped off, not rounded off. This may sometimes lead to an error of 1 degree. For example converting 7 Celsius leads to the evaluation of $7 \times 9 / 5 + 32$. Now $7 \times 9 = 63$, and $63/5 = 12.6$. In integer arithmetic, this is taken to be 12 and, with 32 added to it, gives the final result 44. To the nearest degree the result should be 45.

There is a simple solution to this problem, using the *Java* mathematics class (*Math*) which contains a rounding method. This is called `Math.round()`. We need to amend the *ConvertTemp* class in four places.

First of all, it is no good trying to round `temp` after it has been calculated, because it already has had the decimal fraction part chopped off. We must calculate `temp` with full precision, so amend its declaration to:

```
double    temp = 0;
```

Then we need a variable to hold the value of `temp` as an integer after it has been rounded. Add this line to the variable declarations:

```
int       temp1 = 0;
```

Rounding occurs after the high-precision value of `temp` has been calculated. Insert this line immediately before the printout line:

```
temp1 = Math.round(temp);
```

The `Math.round()` method rounds the value to the nearest whole number and this is assigned to the integer variable, `temp1`. Finally, we alter `temp` in the printout line to `temp1`.

When this method is asked to convert 7 `Celsius`, it gives the correct result, 45 `Fahrenheit`.

What do we mean by 'Equals'?

Testing for equality often uses the symbol `==`. We can write `if (age == 8)`, which returns `true` if `age` equals 8 and returns `false` if `age` has a different value. This symbol is used for *comparisons*. There are other comparison operators such as > (is greater than) and => (is equal to or greater than) as listed on p. 53.

But == is entirely different from the single 'equals' symbol, =. This is used for *assigning* values to variables, as in int age = 8 . The variable age is assigned the value 8.

Comparing the string variables using == is not quite as straightforward as comparing numerical values. For the third 'if' statement in the *ConvertTemp* program we might have written:

```
If (scale == cel)
```

This returns a true value only when scale and cel are the *same object*, that is, stored in the same bytes of memory. But scale and cel were each declared separately as string variables at the beginning of the program. They are *different objects*. The program line above returns false, even when both variables hold identical values.

To compare strings we use the class method called equals (). This takes the two strings and compares them character by character, returning true only if all comparisons yield true. The syntax for using equals is shown in the listing.

The if ... structure

There are three ways of using if...:

1) if (condition) followed by a one-line statement of what is to happen if the condition is true, or by a block of more than one statements enclosed in curly brackets. The condition must be a variable or statement returning a Boolean value (true or false). Nothing happens if the condition is false.

Example:

```
if (age == 8)
name = "Laura";
```

If age is 8, the value Laura is assigned to name. If age is not 8, name retains the value it already has.

39

These two lines make clear the difference between == and =. The conditional operator, ==, makes comparisons, the assignment operator assigns a value.

2) if (condition) followed by a statement or block, followed by else with a statement or block defining what is to happen if the condition is false.

Example:

```
if (age == 8)
name = "Laura";

else if (age == 9)
name =   "Emma";
```

Name is assigned the values Laura or Emma, depending on whether age is 8 or 9, otherwise, it retains its existing value. Note that the 'what to do' lines end in semicolons but the conditional lines do not.

3) if (condition) followed by a statement or block, followed by two or more else if(condition) structures, each with its statement or block of 'what to do' lines.

Example:

```
if (age == 8)
name = "Laura";

else if (age == 9)
name =   "Emma";

else if (age == 10)
name = "Caroline";
```

The conditions are tested one at a time in order and the appropriate action taken if any one or more is true. If none is true, variables retain their existing values.

4) any of the above, but finishing with `else` followed by a statement or block (but no condition). If none of the previous conditions is true, the statement or block is executed and the variables may be given values different from those they initially had.

Example:

```
if (age == 8)
name = "Laura";

else if (age == 9)
name =  "Emma";

else
name = "Name unknown";
```

Try using the `If ...` routine by keying in, running and modifying the following program.

```
class GirlsNames {

        public static void main(String[] args) {

        int age = 0;
        String name = "nobody";

        if (args.length > 0)
                age = Integer.parseInt(args[0]);

        if (age == 8)
                name = "Laura";

        else if (age == 9)
                name =  "Emma";

        else
                name = "unknown";

        System.out.println("The name is " + name);
        }
}
```

You could modify this program to operate on the ages and names of people you know.

For... loops

The ability to repeat an action several times is an important function in many programs. The action may be repeated a given number of times or until a certain condition *becomes* true (using a for... loop) or as long as a certain condition *remains* true (using a while... or do... while... loop).

The structure of a for... loop is:

```
for (starting-value; test; increment) {
    what-to-do statement; }
```

Declaring j as the loop variable, a typical loop is:

```
for (int j = 1; j < 11 ; j = j + 1) {
    System.out.println(j);
    }
```

The values 1 to 10 are printed out on the next ten screen lines. In this example, the loop variable is initialised with the starting-value, 1. Before each loop begins, the test is applied to check that j is less than 11. If the test returns true, the statement is executed; the current value of j is printed on the screen. Then the value of j is incremented by 1. Note that the value of j is **local.** Once the loop has been executed, j ceases to exist. This fact has two consequences: (1) j must be declared every time the loop is initialised; (2) you can use j as the loop variable in several separate loops in a program without the risk of confusing them.

Experiment with using this structure by keying in, running and modifying the program. Make it print numbers from 3 to 12, instead of printing 1 to 10. Modify it to print out the even numbers from 0 to 16. Then try for the multiples of 3 between −14 and + 14.

The for ... loop or its equivalent is used in many languages to provide a delay during the running of a program. We just send the processor running around the loop, doing nothing but taking a certain amount of time to do it. Here is a *Java* version:

```
class waitForMe {

public static void main(String[] args) {

        int limit = 0;
        if (args.length > 0)
        limit = Integer.parseInt(args[0]);

        for (int j = 1; j < limit; j = j + 1) {
                // Do nothing
        }
        System.out.println("Time up!!");
} }
```

Type this in, compile it and run it. It needs a value on the command line to set the number of times the loop is run. Try running it with relatively small values, such as 100 or 200. You will find that it finishes and displays "Time up!!" almost instantaneously. You need to enter large numbers to get an appreciable delay.

Incidentally, you will find that entering a very large number results in an error message and the program stops running. The message tells you that an **exception** has occurred. This is because you have entered a value too big for an integer variable to hold. We have more to say about exceptions later in this chapter and more again in Chapter 10.

Unless you are running a very slow computer, the delays produced by this routine are mostly too short to be of much use. We can increase the delay by nesting a second for ... loop inside the first:

```
class waitLonger {

public static void main(String[] args) {

        int limit = 0;
        if (args.length > 0)
        limit = Integer.parseInt(args[0]);

        for (int j = 1; j < limit; j = j + 1) {
        for (int k = 1; k < limit; k = k + 1) {
                // Do nothing
        }}

        System.out.println("Time up!!");
        }}
```

43

We set the same value for the limit in both loops. This makes the delay roughly proportional to the *square* of the limit. Now we can obtain delays several minutes long.

While... loops

The structure of a while... loop is:

```
while (test) {
      what-to-do statement; }
```

There is no loop variable to be incremented. A while ... loop is useful when the required number of repetitions of the loop is not known in advance.

```
class DataRead1{

public static void main(String[] args) {

      int index = 0;

      if (args.length > 0) {

      while (Integer.parseInt(args[index]) != 99){

      System.out.println(args[index]);
      if (index < (args.length) + 1){
      index = index + 1 ;

} } } } }
```

The program operates on a sequence of values typed on the command line. Note that, in another program, these values could easily come from another source. For example, they might come from the computer's real-time clock or directly from the keyboard. However, at present we are limited to input from the command line. The while... loop runs through the array of values that have been read into and are now stored in args[]. It prints them out in order. The value of index is incremented at each repetition, so as to fetch the next value from args[]. This continues as long as the value is *not* equal (symbol, !=) to 99. The first time that the value is 99, the computer jumps out of the loop without printing the number.

Run this program with various sets of values, to see how it works. There are two cases:

1) A set with 99 occurring in it, but not in first place. Printing stops when the value is 99. *Example:* 1 4 2 8 99 15 32 prints out as 1 4 2 8.

2) A set beginning with 99. There is no printout because the loop condition equals `false` on the first run through. This includes the case where there is only one value (99) in the set. *Example:* 99 6 3 7 12 gives no printout.

The routine does not work if the user forgets to include a 99 in the data. See 'Exceptions' later and in Chapter 10.

The logical structure of this short program is quite complex. The `while...` loop includes an `if...` statement and is itself called by an `if...` statement. Check the brackets with care!

Fig. 13 shows two trial runs of the program.

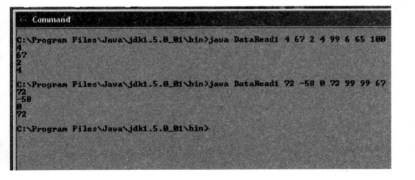

```
Command

C:\Program Files\Java\jdk1.5.0_01\bin>java DataRead1  4 67 2 4 99 6 65 100
4
67
2
4
C:\Program Files\Java\jdk1.5.0_01\bin>java DataRead1  72 -58 0 72 99 99 67
72
-58
0
72
C:\Program Files\Java\jdk1.5.0_01\bin>
```

Fig. 13. Trial runs of DataRead1. *The list of numbers is printed until the computer reaches 99. It can handle zero and negative numbers, but they must be integers.*

45

Do... while... loops

We saw in the previous section that in a while... loop the condition is tested at the *beginning* of each loop. If the condition returns false on the first time round the loop (because it encounters 99), the computer jumps out of the loop without ever executing the 'what-do-do' statement. Otherwise, it prints the numbers in order until it comes to 99. It does not print the 99.

In a do... while... loop, the condition is tested at the *end* of the loop instead of at the beginning. The format is:

> do
> { things to do
> } while (condition);

Here is an example, similar to the previous example, to illustrate the difference in their actions:

```
class DataRead2{

public static void main(String[] args) {

        int index = 0;

if (arguments.length > 0) {

        do
        {System.out.println(args[index]);
        if (index < args.length){
        index++ ;
        } }

        while
(Integer.parseInt(args[index]) != 99);

} } }
```

The do keyword is followed by the 'things-to-do' (print the value and increment index if it has not reached the end of the set). These actions are the same as before, but are now placed *before* the while condition. The while condition is the same as before. There are three cases:

1) A set with 99 occurring in it, but not in first place. Printing stops when the value is 99. *Example:* 1 4 2 8 99 15 32 prints out as 1 4 2 8.

2) The set consists of 99 followed by one or more values, including a second 99. The first 99 is printed but the second is not. This is because the first 99 is printed before the test is applied. The next time 99 occurs, the test detects it and the loop is stopped. *Example:* 99 3 24 7 99 4 5 gives 99 3 24 7.

3) Listing 99 on its own causes 99 to be printed but, then the computer runs on, looking for more values. This happens too when the user forgets to include a 99 in the set. Look at Fig. 14 to see what happens.

Before leaving the subject of while... loops and do... while... loops, note that they can be used instead of for... loops to run for a fixed number of repetitions.

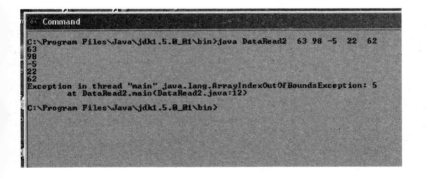

Fig. 14. In trouble! The user has failed to include a 99 on the command line. Consequently, the computer printed the five values and, because there was no 99'to end the sequence, went on to look for a sixth value. There is no such value, so an exception has been thrown.

Exceptions and errors

During compiling or on running some of the earlier programs, you may have received messages about exception errors. These may have occurred as a result of inaccurate keying in. In the while... and do... while... loop programs, an ArrayIndexOutOfBounds exception message occurs when there is no '99' or with only a single '99' in the case of the do... while... loop. Obviously, steps must be taken to avoid these errors, as explained in Chapter 10. However, for the present, we will allow them in these two demonstrations of the action of loops, so as to keep the programming simple.

Things to do

1 Write a program to read a set of values from the command line and then calculate and print out their mean.

2 Write a program to read a series of at least three integer values from the command line, then print out the maximum and minimum values in the set.

3 The while... and do... while... programs throw an exception when 99 is not included in the set. Add a routine to these programs to check through the data *before* it is passed to the loop routines. If 99 is not found, convert the last value in the array to 99, and display a message to warn the user that this has been done.

Summing up Chapters 1 to 5

Java is an **object-oriented** language. The programming unit, or **object**, is a **class**. A class may contain **data** and a **method** (or methods). Methods are short self-contained program segments (also objects) that tell the computer 'what to do'. A class may call on methods defined in other classes.

Classes are defined by typing text into a simple text editor and saving it under the *.java* extension. The file is then compiled by the *javac* program, which saves the compiled version under the same filename but with the *.class* extension. This is run using the *java* program.

A class may include one-line (//) or multi-line (/* ... */) **comments**, that are ignored by the computer. The class definition is **encapsulated** by a statement such as:

```
public class <class name>  {<class definition>}
```

The file *must* be saved under exactly the same class name as given in the definition. The definition usually contains a statement such as:

```
public  static  void  main  (string[]arguments){<data  and
methods>}
```

The keyword `main` indicates to the computer that this definition must be run before any others. A definition may begin by declaring variables and perhaps assign values to them. Then it defines methods to be used by the class. These may include methods that have already been defined in another class. For example:

```
System.out.println ("text");
```

Note the semicolon which indicates that this line is telling the computer to 'do something'. Text may include **escape codes** (p. 21).

There are eight types of variable, including four types of integer variable, all signed: `byte`, `short`, `int`, `long`. Floating-point numbers are stored as `float` or `double`.

Single characters may be stored as `char`. Finally, Boolean variables (the results of logical operations) stored as `boolean`. They can take only two values, `true` and `false` (not 0 and 1, as in some other languages).

The eight types listed above are often called **primitives** because they are an essential built-in feature of *Java*. They are not objects. Strings are declared and used in much the same way as the primitives. Normally a string variable is defined and given a value like this:

```
String warning = "Do not open the valve";
```

However, *String* is not a primitive. It is a class, an object with its own set of methods. Each time we declare a string we create a new instance of the *String* class. Each new string is a new object, but because we need to create strings so often, *Java* does not require us to use `new` to create it. Note that the class identifier, *String*, begins with a capital letter.

Variables are named when defined by using an **identifier**:

```
int height;            (note the semicolon)
```

In this example, the name 'height' is the identifier. Variable names must start with a letter, an underscore or a dollar symbol. By convention, variable names start with a lower-case letter. If the name is made up of several words, subsequent words begin with a capital letter:

```
double timeOfDay;
```

Variables may be assigned a value at the same time as they are defined:

```
int height = 12;
```

Several variables may be declared on a single line:

```
int dividend, divisor, result, remainder;
```

Constants are defined using the keyword `final` before the variable definition:

```
final int speedLimit = 30;
```

We can also use `final` when defining methods and classes. Its effect is that they can not ever be changed (more on p. 118).

Values of variables can be read from the command line using the keyword `arguments` (or its short form, `args`) and allocated to named variables (pp. 33 - 38).

The idea of **instances** is very important in *Java*. Data and methods may be defined for a class as a whole and then the keyword `new` may be used to produce different instances of the class, using different instance values. For example, on p. 23 we created a new instance of the *Divide* class, called *Divide1*. This has its own instance variables and instance methods, identified by prefixing the names defined for the class as a whole with '`Divide1`'.

`Divide1.divisor` and `Divide1.calculate` are examples.

Java includes several useful logical structures, including:

```
            if ...
            for ...
            while ...
            do ... while
```

The `if ...` structure relies on a **condition** which has the form of a Boolean statement. There are three variations on this structure:

```
if (condition)
```
<what to do if condition is true; do nothing if condition is false>;

```
if (condition)
```
 <what to do if condition is true>;
```
else
```
<what to do if condition is false>;

```
if (condition 1)
<what to do if condition 1 is true>;
else if (condition 2)
<what to do if condition 2 is true>;
else if (condition 3)
<what to do if condition 3 is true>;
else if (condition 4)
<what to do if conditon 4 is true>;
else
<what to do if all conditions are false>
```

The 'what to do' lines end with a semicolon, The if, else if, and else lines have no semicolon.

The for ... loop depends on a group of three criteria:

```
for (starting value; test; increment)
{<what to do>; }
```

The items in the condition brackets refer to the **loop variable**. The starting value must declare it and assign it its starting value.The loop variable is **local** and ceases to exist after the loop has been run.

The while ... loop has the form:

```
while (test)
{<what to do>;}
```

This repeats for as long as the test statement is true; it is not executed if the test is false at the first run.

The do ... while loop has this structure:

```
do {<thing to do>} while (condition);
```

This is always executed on the first time round and subsequently, as long as the condition remains true.

Summary tables

1) Operators

Java has more operators than shown in this table, which is limited to the more essential ones.

Type	Operator symbol	Meaning/Example
Assignment	=	age = 25;
Arithmetic	+	add
(returns a numeric	-	subtract
value)	*	multiply
	/	divide
	%	modulus
Comparison	==	equals
(returns a Boolean	!=	does not equal
value)	<	less than
	>	greater than
	<=	less than or equals
	>=	greater than or equals
Logical	&	AND
(returns a Boolean	|	OR
value)	!	NOT
	^	XOR

2) Precedence

In an expression which contains two or more different arithmetic or logical operators, the operators are applied in an order of precedence, as set out in the table below.

Precedence	Operators	Meaning
1	* / %	Multiply, divide, modulus
2	+ -	Add, subtract
3	== !=	Equals, does not equal
4	&	AND
5	^	XOR
6	|	OR

Expressions in brackets are evaluated before expressions outside brackets. If there are nested brackets, the innermost expression is evaluated first.

6 Arrays and other topics

Arrays are a convenient way of handling certain types of data. We can think of an array as a table, such as this one:

Index	Name of day
0	Sunday
1	Monday
2	Tuesday
3	Wednesday
4	Thursday
5	Friday
6	Saturday

The table has room for seven entries, one for each day of the week. The rows of the table are indexed, but note that (in *Java*) the index runs from 0 to 6, not from 1 to 7.

One advantage of placing data (names of weekdays) in a table (or array) is that we need only one name (nameOfDay) for the array, and can refer to any one of the entries by quoting its index. Thus, nameOfDay[4] is Thursday. This may not seem much of an advantage for handling single weekdays but it does lend itself to processing data. We could process the names is some way, using a For . . . loop to perform that same operation on each of the names in turn. This is much simpler to program that processing each of the seven days individually. Later, we will look at a program that uses this technique.

Before looking at the program, there are a few general points to consider. The first is that an array can hold only one type of data. The array above holds string variables. Another array might hold integers. But no array can hold both strings and integers.

Arrays are declared in either of two ways. The array above could be declared by:

```
String[]      nameOfDay;
```

or by:

```
String        nameOfDay[];
```

At this stage the identifier of the array has been declared but the length of the array (the number of items of data that it can hold) and its content have not.

The length can be defined by using the keyword new:

```
String []     nameOfDay = new String[7]
```

The content of the array is not yet defined, so each item is automatically given an initial value. This is "" in the case of String arrays, 0 in numeric arrays and False in Boolean arrays.

To create an array directly and load data into it, we simply list the content:

```
String[]  nameOfDay  =   {"Sunday",   "Monday",
"Tuesday",  "Wednesday",  "Thursday",  "Friday",
"Saturday"}
```

This technique applies only to *String* arrays, because only *String* objects can be initialised without using new. We can now understand what is happening behind the scenes in the program on p. 33. When the program is run, *Java* automatically creates a *String[]* array called args and reads the data on the command line into it, as strings. In that program we convert the strings into integers before processing them numerically.

Note the use of the variable args.length. When an array is created, a corresponding integer variable is set up automatically to hold the number of items in the array. In the program, args.length is equal to 3. In the previous example nameOfDay.length is equal to 7. Later, we shall see other examples of using the length variable.

Using arrays

Here is a simple array-based program, called *dayNumber*.

```
class dayNumber {
public static void main(String[] args) {

        String[] ordinalNumber =
        {"first","second","third","fourth","fifth",
        "sixth","seventh"};

        String[] dayOfWeek =
        {"Sunday","Monday","Tuesday",
        "Wednesday","Thursday","Friday","Saturday"};

        int     select = 0;

        if (args.length > 0)
                        select =
        Integer.parseInt(args[0]) - 1;

        System.out.println("The " + ordinalNumber[select]
        + " day of the week is " + dayOfWeek[select] +
        ".");
}}
```

There are several long lines in this listing. The semicolons show exactly where the *program* lines end.

The program accepts input of a single integer, which must lie between 1 and 7. This is taken to be the day of the week, with Sunday being Day 1.

The computer responds by displaying a statement. For example, if the input digit is '4', the display reads "The fourth day of the week is Wednesday."

The way the program works is this. It begins by creating and initializing two string arrays, each with seven entries. There is ordinalNumber[], which holds ordinal numbers from "first" to "seventh", and there is dayOfWeek[], which holds the names of the days from "Sunday" to "Saturday". The program also creates an integer variable called select, the number of the selected day.

The method of this class checks that there is in fact an integer on the command line. If so, it looks at the first string in the arguments array and converts it into an integer, stored in select. This value is then used to pick out the corresponding pair of entries from the ordinalNumber[] and the dayOfWeek[] arrays and insert them in the display message.

The appropriate item is selected from each array by using select as the index number. However this is not quite as simple as it seems because the locations in the *Java* arrays are indexed from 0 upward. By contrast, the days of the week are numbered from 1 to 7 and the ordinal numbers run from "first" to "seventh". This is why we subtract 1 from select before using it to index the arrays.

This program illustrates how organizing data into arrays is so helpful when handling systematically arranged data.

More arrays

This program uses arrays of integers:

```
class nutsAndBolts {

public static void main(String[] args) {

int[]   unitPrice = { 2, 5, 4 };
int[]   partCost = new int[3];
int     quantity = 0;
int     totalCost = 0;

if (args.length > 2)
for (int j = 0; j < 3; j = j + 1) {
        quantity = Integer.parseInt(args[j]);
        partCost[j] = quantity * unitPrice[j];
        totalCost = totalCost + partCost[j];
        }
```

```
System.out.println("The total cost is " + totalCost);

}}
```

This program calculates the total cost of quantities of nuts, bolts and washers, each commodity having a different unit price. The quantities are specified by typing three integers on the command line.

The unit prices (in pence) are initialised when the array `unitPrice` is declared. Another array is declared, without values initialised, to hold the costs for nuts, bolts and washers respectively. Each entry in this array will eventually hold the cost of the given quantity of each commodity.

The program checks that there are at least 3 quantities specified and, if so, enters a typical `for . . .` loop to process the three commodities in order. The program is simplified by using arrays, for we can identify the commodities by the loop index `j`, which is also used to index the entries in the arrays.

Each time round the loop the computer:

1 Reads the quantity from `args []`,
2 Calculates the part-cost by multiplying the quantity by the unit price, and
3 Cumulatively sums the part-costs to find the total cost for nuts, bolts and washers.

It is interesting to contrast the syntax of the lines that create the integer arrays. Array `unitPrice []` is created directly with values that are already known. The values are not known for `partCost []`, so an empty array with three locations is created:

```
int[] partCost = new int[3];
```

This line is creating the array as a new instance of the integer array `int []`. Note again that the double square brackets can be after the `int` on the left or after the `partCost`.

59

Converting data types

This operation is referred to as **casting**. Just as we can melt down a glass bottle in a foundry and cast it into a different shape, so we can cast an integer variable, stored as a `byte`, into a `long`. It retains its numeric value, just as the new object is still glass after it has been cast.

Before discussing casting in more detail, we will summarise the types of data that exist in *Java*. The table below lists the eight primitives and the range of values that they can have:

Type of variable	Defining keyword	Range
Integer	`byte`	−128 to 127
	`short`	−32 768 to 32 767
	`int`	−2E31 to 2E31 − 1
	`long`	−2E63 to 2E63 − 1
Floating point	`float`	1.4E−45 to 3.4E+38
	`double`	4.9E−324 to 1.7E+308
Single character	`char`	alphanumeric symbols and punctuation, etc.
Boolean	`boolean`	true or false

Because Boolean variables have only two opposite values, which are not numerical, it is not possible to cast any of the other types into Boolean form.

Integer types can be cast from one to the other, provided that the type we cast into has a range that includes the value we wish to store. To be certain, it is best if we always cast from a type of smaller range into one of greater range. For example, there are no problems in casting a `byte` into an `int`, or a `short` into a `long`. Casting of these types is automatic. For example, you can use an `int` as a `long` without needing to specify the change.

If a casting does not occur automatically, we can cast by using a statement such as this:

```
(type)value
```

For example:

```
(double)accountTotal
```

This casts `accountTotal` as a `double`. The same format can be used with an expression, for example:

```
(int)(unitCost * quantity - discount)
```

This evaluates the expression and then stores the result as an integer. Note the brackets around the expression. This is because casting takes precedence higher than that of mathematical operations. If the expression were unbracketed the casting would apply only to its first term (`unitCost`). The result might have a different numerical value and might also be a different type, such as `float`.

Casting may also done with objects, such as instances of a class, but this is beyond the scope of this book. However, there is one common object type, `String`, that we have already cast in several of our examples. All input, including numeric values, is read from the command line into the string array, `args[]`.

Often we need to cast the numeric values on the command line as integers. This is the function of a method of the `Integer` class, called `Integer.parseInt()`.

There are several examples of this on previous pages.

The *Limerick* program (below) has examples of casting a `double` as an `int`. It is used there as a simple way of *chopping off* the fractional part of the value of the `double`. This is not the same as *rounding* it off. For example, rounding the value 3.5 gives 4, but casting a `double` of value 3.5 gives an `int` with value 3.

Java **verse**

Now we look at an example of casting and take the subject of arrays a stage further. The next class, *Limerick,* is a light-hearted foray into handling arrays. Before we study the program, there is another aspect of arrays to cover. This is the subject of **multidimensional arrays**. Readers who have used BASIC will be familiar with a command such as DIM A$(4, 5). This creates a 2-dimensional string array called A$, with 4 rows and 5 columns. Each of the 20 strings in the array can be identified by using its two indices.

Java does not have multidimensional arrays, but it is easy to program the equivalent by defining an **array of arrays**. For example, to set up the equivalent of DIM A$(4,5), we type:

```
String [] [] A$ = new String[4][5]
```

This creates a new array with four locations, each of which holds a string array with five locations. We use this procedure in the *Limerick* program opposite.

Limerick composes verse by randomly selecting words and phrases that are stored in arrays. The arrays have the identifiers wordA, wordB, wordC ... wordI. First, it directly defines six of these arrays, each having two, three or four locations.

WordD requires three arrays, each with two locations. This is defined according to the technique described above. Then the six locations are filled with strings.

WordF is similar, but requires two arrays, each with three locations.

Remember that the locations are numbered from 0 upward, but the numbers in square brackets specify the actual numbers of locations that the array has. So WordF is initialised as new String[2][3] and has six locations, wordF[0][0] to wordF[1][2].

```
class Limerick {
public static void main (String[] args) {

String[] wordA = {"poor", "fat", "rich"};
String[] wordB = {"singer", "writer", "toddler", "pop
star"};
String[] wordC = {"Andrew", "Sarah", "Winnie"};
String[] wordE = {"one day", "one night"};
String[] wordG = {"silly", "hopeless"};
String[] wordH = {"always", "seldom"};
String[] wordI = {"went out", "started"};

String[][] wordD = new String[3][2];
wordD[0][0] = "liked eating cheese fondue";
wordD[0][1] = "said 'Yes' and then 'Can do'";
wordD[1][0] = "ate steak so much rarer";
wordD[1][1] = "thought no one would dare 'er";
wordD[2][0] = "liked wearing a pinny";
wordD[2][1] = "looked horribly skinny";

String [][] wordF = new String[2][3];
wordF[0][0] = "romp in the hay";
wordF[0][1] = "join in the fray";
wordF[0][2] = "go out to play";
wordF[1][0] = "have a good fight";
wordF[1][1] = "put out the light";
wordF[1][2] = "just be polite";

int randA = (int)(Math.random() * 3);
int randB = (int)(Math.random() * 4);
int randC = (int)(Math.random() * 3);
int randD = (int)(Math.random() * 2);
int randE = (int)(Math.random() * 2);
int randF = (int)(Math.random() * 3);
int randG = (int)(Math.random() * 2);
int randH = (int)(Math.random() * 2);
int randI = (int)(Math.random() * 2);

System.out.println("\nThere was a " + wordA[randA] + " "
 + wordB[randB] + " called " + wordC[randC] + ",");
System.out.println("Who " + wordH[randH] + " " +
 wordD[randC][randD]);
System.out.println("And " + wordI[randI]
 + " " + wordE[randE] + ',');
System.out.println("To " + wordF[randE][randF] + ",");
System.out.println("That " + wordG[randG] + " "
+ wordA[randA] + " " + wordB[randB] + " called "
 + wordC[randC] + ".");
}}
```

63

The fourth block of statements in the program produces nine random numbers to be used to select words from the arrays.

Note the technique for generating randA. This is to be a **random integer** ranging from 0 to 2, used to select one of the locations in wordA. The call to Math.Random produces a value between 0 and 0.999.... When this is multiplied by 3, it ranges from 0 to 2.999...., but not 3. The (Math.random() * 3) expression is enclosed in brackets to **cast** into an integer variable randA, using:

```
(int)(Math.random() * 3)
```

When cast as an int, it loses the digits to the right of the decimal point, so its range comprises only the three integers 0, 1, and 2. This is an example of non-automatic casting, as described on p. 61.

The final stage of the program consists of five statements to print the five lines of *Limerick*. Note the use of the escape code \n, to introduce a blank line before the printout of the verse.

```
c:\ Command

C:\Program Files\Java\jdk1.5.0_01\bin>java Limerick

There was a poor pop star called Winnie,
Who always looked horribly skinny
And started one night,
To have a good fight,
That hopeless poor pop star called Winnie.

C:\Program Files\Java\jdk1.5.0_01\bin>java Limerick

There was a fat singer called Andrew,
Who seldom said 'Yes' and then 'Can do'
And went out one day,
To go out to play,
That silly fat singer called Andrew.

C:\Program Files\Java\jdk1.5.0_01\bin>
```

Fig. 15. Limerick *combines the words entirely at random in 3456 different ways, so you are unlikely to get exactly the same verse twice.*

Sorting numbers

When sorting numbers it is essential to have a systematic way of handling them. This is another useful application of arrays. The *sorter* program listed below demonstrates a useful way of doing this. The method used `Arrays.sort()`:

```
import java.util.*;

class sorter {

public static void main(String[] args) {

int[] values = new int[args.length];

for (int j = 0; j < args.length; j = j + 1) {
                values[j] = Integer.parseInt(args[j]);
        }
for (int j = 0; j < args.length; j = j + 1) {
                System.out.println(values[j]);
        }
System.out.println(Arrays.toString(values));

Arrays.sort(values);

System.out.println(Arrays.toString(values));

}}
```

We begin by importing the utility package (p. 124) because the specialised methods for processing arrays are part of this. Then the main method creates an array called `values[]` to hold the values that the user has typed on the command line. A `for ...` loop reads in these values, they are converted to integers and stored in the `values[]` array.

Next comes the second `for ...` loop which prints out the stored values individually. This is included only to show the contents of `values[]`, and could be omitted from the program.

Now we make use of a method which was introduced in the new version 1.5.0 of *Java 2*, commonly referred to as *J2SE 5* or *Tiger*. This new `Arrays.toString()` method prints out the contents of the array as a single string, instead of individually. This avoids the complications of a `for ...` loop.

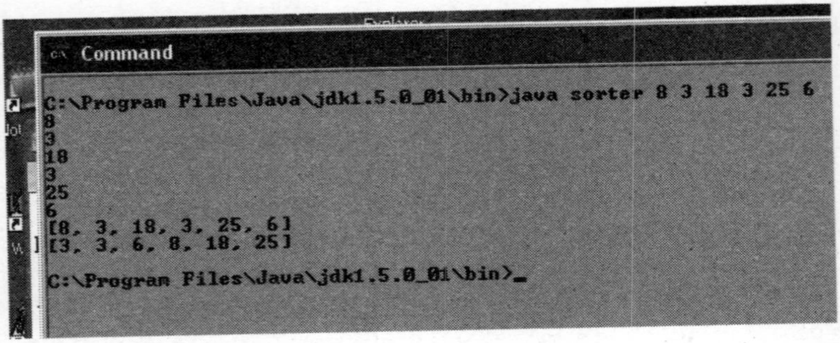

Fig. 16. Demonstrating the use of the `Arrays.toString()` *and the* `Arrays.sort()` *methods.*

Sorting into ascending numerical order is easily achieved by calling:

```
Arrays.sort(values)
```

Finally, we use `Arrays.toString()` again to print out the sorted values. The result of a typical run of the program appears in Fig. 16. First we have the individual values listed one below the other. Then they are displayed as a single string in square brackets. After sorting, they are displayed in their sorted order.

The sorting method can also be used with the `binarySearch()` method, as illustrated by this program:

```
import java.util.*;

class pickOut {

public static void main(String[] args) {

int [] values = new int [args.length];

for (int j = 0; j < args.length; j = j + 1) {
            values[j] = Integer.parseInt(args[j]);
        }

Arrays.sort(values);
int place = Arrays.binarySearch(values, 10);
```

66

```
System.out.println(place);
}}
```

This accepts several integers typed on the command line before running. It sorts them into ascending numerical order. Then the method binarySearch is applied to the sorted array. The second parameter specifies the number to search for. In this program it is 10. The method returns the position of the value 10 in the sorted array. Here the position is assigned to the variable place.

Another array printing method

If printing out the contents of an array is complicated, it becomes even more complicated when the array has two or more dimensions, as in the *Limerick* program (p. 62-4). *Tiger* has come to the rescue with a new method for printing multidimensional arrays, deepToString().

```
import java.util.*;

class timesTable {

public static void main(String[] args) {

int [] [] series = new int[3][5];

for (int j = 0; j < 3; j = j + 1) {

        for (int k = 0; k < 5; k = k + 1) {

                series[j][k] = (j + 1) * k;
        }}

System.out.println(Arrays.deepToString(series));

}}
```

Before using deepToString(), this program has two nested for . . . loops to fill the series[] [] two-dimensional array. The array holds three series of five integers each. They are then printed out by the new method.

Comparing arrays

It is sometimes useful to be able to compare two arrays to determine whether or not their contents are identical. For one-dimensional arrays, this is done by using `Arrays.equals()`. This is different from the `equals` described on p. 38. The brackets hold two parameters, the names of the two arrays. For example:

```
if (Arrays.equals(arrayA, arrayB)) {
        appropriate action
}
```

testEm demonstrates its action on three one-dimensional arrays:

```
import java.util.*;

class testEm {
public static void main(String[] args) {

String[] oneWayA = {"a", "b", "c", "d"};
String[] oneWayB = {"a", "p", "c", "d"};
String[] oneWayC = {"a", "b", "c", "d"};

if (Arrays.equals(oneWayA, oneWayB)) {
        System.out.println("A & B are equal");
}
else {
        System.out.println("A & B are NOT equal");
}
if (Arrays.equals(oneWayA, oneWayC)) {
        System.out.println("A & C are equal");
}
else {
        System.out.println("A & C are NOT equal");
}
}}
```

Three sample string arrays are declared, using the technique described on p. 56. We then compare `oneWayA` with `oneWayB`, using:

```
        if (Arrays.equals(oneWayA, oneWayB))
```

The expression in brackets yields a Boolean result, which is either true or false. If the expression is true then "A & B are equal" is displayed on the screen. Otherwise, the display reads "A & B are NOT equal".

Another array method, new with *Tiger*, extends the capability of `Arrays.equals()` from single-dimension to multidimension arrays. The method is called `Arrays.deepEquals()`. See 'Things To Do' item 5, below for further details.

Things to do

1 Using the `dayNumber` class as an example, design a program that displays selected   lines from the poem "Monday's child is fair of face".

2 Expand the *nutsAndBolts* program so that it displays a complete invoice for the sale of nuts, bolts and washers. The invoice is to show for each commodity, the quantity ordered, the unit cost and the cost of that quantity of the commodity. It also shows the total cost.

3 Write your own version of *Limerick*. It is more fun if you base it on the names of relatives and friends. Remember to make the appropriate lines rhyme and scan correctly.

4 Try the *pickOut* program, giving it integer values that do not include 10. Also try it with arrays that include 10 more than once. Can you find any rules that determine the value given to `place`?

5 Write a program to compare three 2-dimensional arrays, two at a time. Model the program on *testEm*, opposite. You can declare the sample arrays either as in *Limerick* (p. 63) or directly, as on p. 56. For example, a 2 by 4 array can be declared like this:

```
String[][]   twoWayA   =   {{"a",   "b",   "c",
"d"},{"e", "f", "g", "h"}};
```

7 A new look

In this chapter, we introduce two new ways of getting into contact with the program. Until now we have used the command window. To input data, we have typed one or more arguments after the filename (see Fig.11, p. 35). To output data, we have included program lines of the `System.out.println()` type.

Now we move a little closer to the methods of input and output used by the computer's operating system. The examples are based on a PC running *Windows XP*, but similar results are obtainable with other systems.

Run-time input

The routine below uses a method belonging to the *swing* package. This contains a large number of classes dealing with display routines. To make these classes available to our program we begin with the command `import javax.swing.*`. The asterisk indicates that we are importing all the *swing* classes. This is not strictly necessary in this case, since we are using only one class from the package.

```
import javax.swing.*;

public class newInput
{
        public static void main(String[] args)
        {
                String value = JOptionPane.showInputDialog
("Key in a number");

                int numberValue = Integer.parseInt(value);

                System.out.println("The number is " +
numberValue);

                System.exit(0);
}        }
```

Key in this class and compile it in the usual way. Then type `java newInput` and press Enter. A window appears on the screen, as illustrated in Fig. 17.

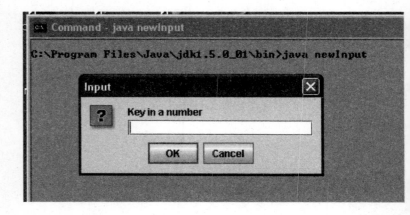

Fig. 17. The window created by using newInput *has the typical* Windows *format. You can drag it around the screen, as we have done here to centre it just below the command line.*

The imported class is *JOptionPane,* and the method is `showInputDialog()`. This defines a small window containing text (defined by the argument) and a space into which data (an integer value) can be typed. There are 'OK' and 'Cancel' buttons.

The user types in a number, which appears in the window. The typed data is returned as a string, the value of which is assigned to the integer variable, `numberValue`. The next line displays the value on the command screen, and clears the small window from the display as soon as the user presses Enter.

This program needs a final line, `System.exit(0)`, to return it to the operating system.

Output

Programming for output is more complicated than for input, but here is a fairly simple routine that displays a window containing a text message.

```
import javax.swing.*;

public class outFrame }
        public static void main(String[] args)
        {
                JFrame message = new JFrame();
                message.setDefaultCloseOperation(JFrame.
EXIT_ON_CLOSE);
                JLabel messageLabel = new JLabel("This is
the message");

                JPanel panel = new JPanel();
                panel.add(messageLabel);
                message.setContentPane(panel);
                message.pack();
                message.show();
}}
```

The aim of the program is to create and display a frame containing a message. As in the previous program, we need to use several classes from the swing package, so we begin by importing it.

The class listing begins by creating a new instance of *JFrame*, called *message*. The next line ensures that the program remains running until the frame is closed. Then we set out the message that is to be displayed, and call it messageLabel.

The remaining lines are concerned with putting the display elements together. First we create a new instance of *JPanel* called *panel*. Then we add messageLabel to *panel* and set it as the content of the frame. To finalise the operation we pack the frame and show it. The pack method automatically adjusts the size of the frame to fit the items that are in it. Until the final command, show(), is given the frame is invisible. We do not show it until all the components of it have been put together. The result is shown in Fig. 18. Usually the frame appears at the top left corner of the screen, but we dragged it away for the illustration.

73

Fig. 18. The display frame obtained by running outFrame.

Like us, you may think that pack() is cramming the text into too small a frame. If so, delete the pack() expression from the program and substitute:

```
message.setSize(200,200);
```

The numbers represent the width and depth of the frame in pixels. Recompile the program as *outFrame1* and run it. Fig. 19 is the result.

Fig. 19. By using setSize() instead of pack(), you can make the frame any size you like. It can even fill the whole screen.

Depending on what version of *Java* you are running, you may have noted an on-screen warning when compiling outFrame with *javac*. This did not prevent *javac* from compiling the program properly. Also, it did not prevent *java* from running the program and showing the desired result. The purpose of the warning is to tell you that one of the APIs you have used is **deprecated**. The API (Application Programming Interface — a method or class) is OK, but there is now a newer (and presumably better) way of doing things. You can ignore the warning and then search the latest books (and the website) to discover the better way.

The warning informed us that the show() method used in outFrame is now deprecated. There is something better that we can use. As explained in detail in Chapter 10, we found that the better method is setVisible(). This takes a Boolean argument. If the argument is true, the window is displayed. If the argument is false, the window is hidden. The next program shows this happening:

```
import javax.swing.*;
public class bugAlert {

        public static void main(String[] args){
                boolean delay = true;

                JFrame message = new JFrame();

        message.setDefaultCloseOperation(JFrame.EXIT_
ON_CLOSE);
                JLabel messageLabel = new JLabel("DANGER!
BUGS ATTACKING!!");

                JPanel panel = new JPanel();
                panel.add(messageLabel);
                message.setContentPane(panel);
                message.setSize(200, 200);

                while (delay = true) {
                for (int j = 1; j < 10000; j = j + 1) {
                for (int k = 1; k < 10000; k = k + 1) {
                }}
                message.setVisible(true);
                for (int j = 1; j < 20000; j = j + 1) {
                for (int k = 1; k < 20000; k = k + 1) {
                }}
                message.setVisible(false);

}}}
```

Minor differences between this program and *outFrame* are:

- This program is called *bugAlert* and, for this reason, the message has been changed to something appropriate.
- A Boolean variable `delay` is initialised and given the value `true`.
- It uses the larger panel as seen in Fig. 19.

The main difference between the programs is seen in the last block of coding, starting with the `while...` loop. The loop repeats for as long as (`delay = true`). Because `delay` has already been set to `true` and the program never changes it, the loop repeats for ever.

Inside the loop is the routine for making the message visible and invisible alternately. To do this we use the `message.setVisible()` method. It is first of all made true, so the message appears. Then there is a delay caused by the `for ...` `loop` as described on p. 43. After this, the message is made invisible and there is another delay. This visible-delay-invisible-delay sequence is repeated indefinitely because it is inside the `while ...` loop.

When *bugAlert* is run, the warning message flashes on and off at the top left corner of the screen. To stop it, either click on the 'close' button at the top right corner of the message window, or close the command screen.

Unicode characters

You are already looking at Unicode characters because they include all the alphabetical and numerical characters, punctuation and many other symbols (such as €) that we frequently see in everyday text.

The Unicode characters include all these and very many more. To look at some of the less common ones, reload the *outFrame* program (p. 73) and edit it to display a different 'message'. First, type in an extra line at the beginning of the main method (just before 'JFrame message ...'):

```
char code = (char) 0x0E2D;
```

76

This is a way of representing a character as a number. The format of the number, which is preceded by '0x' indicates to *Java* that this is a hexadecimal number. Every unicode character has a hexadecimal number to identify it. What this line is doing is to declare a char variable named code and give it the value obtained by casting (see pp. 60-1) the hexadecimal number as a char. We will see the purpose of this in a moment.

The second amendment to the program is to delete the message, "This is the message" and replace it with:

```
"\u00A5  " + code + "  \u27A1"
```

This message consists of three Unicode characters, which we can see when the JFrame is displayed.

To complete the editing, change the class name from *outFrame* to *unic*, and save the file under a new filename, unic.java. Compile the program, then run it. Fig. 20 shows the result.

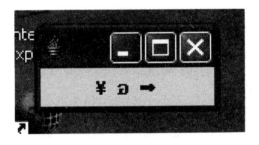

*Fig. 20. Examples of Unicode characters.
The symbol for the Japanese currency unit,
the yen; a letter from the Thai alphabet; a
right-pointing arrow symbol.*

Until the recent introduction of Unicode version 4.0, the previous collection of characters was defined by a 4-digit hexadecimal. This gave it the possibility of defining 65536 different characters represented by numbers from 0000 to FFFF. The first 127 were the standard ASCII characters, mainly upper-case and lower-case letters, numerals and punctuation. Now the code covers the alphabets and symbols of dozens of languages from Greek and Thai to Devanagari and Bengali. Among the symbols covered, probably the most generally useful are the mathematical symbols. However there are numerous other symbols such as 'smileys', musical notes, Braille patterns and Dingbats (see item 6 under 'Things To Do', p. 80).

More recently, Unicode version 4.0 was released and the latest version of *Java* (1.5.0, or *Tiger)* has been updated to support all the new symbols now included. These have 5-digit hexadecimal numbers in the range from 10000 to 1FFFF. The char type can cope only with 4-digit numbers so methods have been introduced that use integer variables. The characters in the extended range are mainly of very specialised use. For example, they include the characters of Linear B script, which would be of interest only to professional archaeologists.

Input and Output

Now we combine both techniques in the same program. Compare *Birthday* (see listing opposite) with the previous examples, *newInput* (p. 71) and *outFrame* (p. 73).

The class needs to import *swing* classes and methods, so the first line does this. As usual, we do not bother to indicate which of the classes and methods of *swing* that we need. The asterisk is a 'wild card' that means 'any class or method', so the whole of the *swing* package is imported. There is more about *Java* packages and their importance in Chapter 11.

The program then asks for two data inputs, the current year and the birth year. These are received as strings, but converted to integers in the usual way. Then comes a line in which these two values are used to calculate the output value, age.

78

```java
import javax.swing.*;

public class Birthday {

        int current = 0;
        int birth = 0;


        public static void main(String[] args)
        {
                String thisYear =
JOptionPane.showInputDialog("Key in the current year");
                int current = Integer.parseInt(thisYear);
                String birthYear =
JOptionPane.showInputDialog("Key in your birth year");
                int birth = Integer.parseInt(birthYear);

                int age = current - birth;

                JFrame message = new JFrame();
                message.setDefaultCloseOperation(JFrame.
EXIT_ON_CLOSE);
                JLabel messageLabel = new JLabel("This year
you are " + age + " years old.");
                JPanel panel = new JPanel();
                panel.add(messageLabel);
                message.setContentPane(panel);
                message.pack();
                message.setVisible(true);

}}
```

The third stage of the program is the same as the *outFrame* class, except for the message. The argument of messageLabel comprises text strings and an integer value. When strings and integers are concatenated like this, *Java* automatically casts the integers as strings.

This is a very basic program. The input and output windows are not well laid out and their screen positions are not ideal. Also, we have not made any provision for the user who clicks on the 'Cancel' button. But this is a useful routine if you are wanting to write and test mathematical operations.

In Chapters 14 and 15, we will show how to improve its visual aspects, and how to set the fonts and the colours.

Things to do

1 Define a class called *myName* which asks the user to type in their full name (given names followed by family name) and then prints it on the command screen.

2 Extend the class above to ask for the full name, then print out the given names and family name on separate lines on the command screen.

3 Invent a class that displays a succession of frames at 5-second intervals, quoting successive lines in a well-known song or poem.

4 Write programs with screen input and output, based on the structure of the `Birthday` class. Possible topics are:
a) converting pounds sterling to US dollars, given the current exchange rate.
b) calculating the current in amps through a resistor, given its resistance in ohms and the voltage across it (Note: current = voltage/resistance). A simple program could use integers, but using `double` variables and rounding off to three decimal places (nearest milliamp) would improve it.

5 Invent a class that plays a simple game called *Guess The Number*. It displays a panel on the screen asking the player to key in any number between 0 and 9. The class then generates a random integer in the range 0 to 9. If this is the same as the number typed in by the player a frame is displayed saying "You win!". Otherwise a frame appears saying "Sorry, you lost."

6 Amend the *unic* program to display other characters. You can identify them either by declaring a `char` variable such as `code` or by using the escape character "\u". Try putting in any values you like and seeing what you get. If you want to find the codes for particular characters, go to the Unicode website, where they are all listed:

www.unicode.org

8 OOP in action

In the previous seven chapters we have looked at many (though by no means all) of the things that *Java* can do. We have seen how to use the keywords and program structures to perform quite complicated tasks. We have written programs, some short, some long. Yet, are these programs object orientated? Almost all of them are essentially *procedural* (see Fig. 1, p. 2), just like like programs written in BASIC or some other procedural language. They use *Java* keywords and structures and are wrapped up in a class definition, but they are still procedural. Where are the objects?

This query overlooks that fact that we have certainly employed quite a number of objects in our programs. In our first program we called the method `System.out.println()`. This may look like a rather fancy keyword but in fact it is a call to an object written by someone else and stored in the the library of objects (APIs) provided with the *Java Development Kit*. Looking through the other programs, you will note many other objects that we have used. Examples of these objects include: `String`, `StringTokenizer`, `args.length`, and `JOptionPane`. So we *have* been using OOP after all!

Now we take it further. The reason for this is to simplify our programs, to make them more reliable and testable, and to make them really flexible and useful. Then we shall be reaping the benefit of using *Java*.

A procedural program

All programs are procedural to a certain extent, except those with only one program line. If there are two or more lines, it is procedural. However there is no great objection to short procedures. It is when it gets to 20 or more lines that we begin to worry that it would be better to reduce the length.

Such a program is *motion*, listed on pp. 27-8. Its procedure can be summarised as follows:

- Declare the six variables.
- Method workItOut() shows how to calculate final-Speed and distance, given initialSpeed, accel and time.
- Method Printout() displays a statement of the car's final speed and distance travelled.
- Then comes the main method which begins by creating an instance of *motion*, called *OldBanger*.
- The variables of *OldBanger* are given values.
- workItOut() is called to calculate finalSpeed and distance.
- Printout() is called to display the result.
- The previous 4 stages are repeated to create a new instance of *motion*, called *SoupedUp*.

This program did not take its input from the keyboard, so keyboard input would be a useful addition to the program. It requires an extra stage at the beginning of the program, which would make it longer than it is already, so we will write this as a separate program. To do this we create a new class, but call it *motionInput*. This is the listing:

```
import javax.swing.*;

public class motionInput
{
        float initialSpeed;
        float accel;
        float time;

        public void keyInData()
        {
                String value0 = JOptionPane.showInputDialog
("Initial speed? (m/s)");
                initialSpeed = Float.parseFloat(value0);

                String value1 = JOptionPane.showInputDialog
("Acceleration? (m/s/s)");
                accel = Float.parseFloat(value1);

                String value2 = JOptionPane.showInputDialog
("Time? (s)");
                time = Float.parseFloat(value2);

}        }
```

This class is like the class *newInput*, which is listed on p. 71. It begins by importing all the swing classes, so that we can set up small panels to receive the input. In *motionInput* there are three panels, one for initial speed, one for acceleration and one for time. They are displayed one at a time and each stays on the screen until a value is keyed in.

The values are assigned to the variables initialSpeed, accel, and time. Note that the values are asigned to floating-point variables, using a method called Float.parseFloat(). This is similar to the method Integer.parseInt(), which we have often used for reading data from the command line.

If you key in this class, save it, and then compile it with *javac*, everything goes as usual. However, if you try to run the .class file, using *java*, an exception message is displayed and the class does not run. This is because the class has no main method. It has a class method, keyInData(), but no main method. The computer can not find anywhere to start running.

What we have here is a general-purpose routine for entering data about the motion of an old banger, a souped-up car, or any other vehicle that we can think of. But to use this routine we have to develop another class.

Extending the class

The class *motionInput* is not much use on its own. We need to tell the computer what to do with the data that has recently been typed in. This is the function of another class, called *workItOut*:

```
class workItOut extends motionInput {

        float finalSpeed = 0;
        float distance = 0;

        public void workOutSpeed() {
        finalSpeed = initialSpeed + accel * time;
        distance = (initialSpeed + finalSpeed) / 2 *
time;

}}
```

The first line states that this class extends the *motionInput* class. It is a continuation of that class. Objects belonging to *motionInput* are accessible to *workItOut*. We say that *workItOut* **inherits** the variables and methods of *motionInput*. **Inheritance** is an important feature of *Java*. The features of a given class are available to all its sub-classes. In this example, the variables that are typed in when *motionInput* is running are available to be used by *workItOut*, when it is calculating finalSpeed and distance.

Putting it together

Although we have extended *motionInput* by adding some calculation methods, we still have not provided a main method. The computer still can find nowhere to begin. This comes in a third class called *vehicleMotion*:

```
class vehicleMotion{
public static void main(String[] args) {

        workItOut car = new workItOut();

        car.keyInData();

        car.workOutSpeed();

        System.out.println("\nFinal speed = " +
car.finalSpeed + " m/s.");
        System.out.println("Distance = " + car.distance +
" m.");
}}
```

This is quite a short class but at least it has a main method. The computer can run it!

The first thing in *vehicleMotion* is to create a new instance of the *workItOut* class, called *car*. We could, of course, create other instances too, as when we created *oldBanger* and *soupedUp*, but there is no need for this in this version of the *motion* program. Now that we can type in data for each kind of vehicle, instead of the values being already specified in the program, we do not need to create an instance for each type of vehicle.

84

In the orginal *motion* class, on pp. 27-8, we created two new instances of the *motion* class itself. In this version, the *vehicleMotion* class, we create not a new instance of *vehicleMotion*, but a new instance of *workItOut*. This links the two classes. It tells the computer where to go to find the method for working out the calculations. Also, because *workItOut* extends *motionInput*, it tells the computer where to find the method for keying in the data.

Now to return to the description of running *vehicleMotion*. The next stage in *vehicleMotion* is to call keyInData, using the statement:

```
car.keyInData;
```

This takes the computer back through *workItOut* to the keyInData method of *motionInput*. A sequence of three input panels is displayed on the screen and the user is invited to enter the data.

That done, the next line of *vehicleMotion* is:

```
car.workOutSpeed
```

This is the method that is part of *workItOut*. Two new variables are declared and then the method workOutSpeed calculates final-Speed and distance. The computer then returns to its main method in *vehicleMotion* and displays the two calculated values on the command screen.

Advantages

The way that the three classes work together (Fig. 21) may be difficult to understand, and you might wonder why we prefer this to the single procedural class listed on pp. 27-8. One advantage is that *motionInput* is a short class, easy to write, easy to understand, easy to debug, and easy to modify if we want to improve it later. The same applies even more to its extension, *workItOut*.

85

In addition, *vehicleMotion* consists mainly of calls to variable declarations and methods that are in the other two classes. These calls need only a line each, yet each result in a relatively complicated sequence of actions. Because they each occupy a single line (rarely more) it is easy for the reader to see exactly what the computer is doing and in what order. The structure of the program is clear. These considerations explain why *Java* is such a popular language, even if its object orientated approach is unfamiliar and difficult to understand at first encounter.

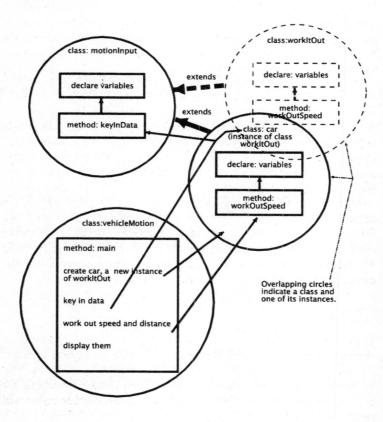

Fig. 21. The relationships between the objects that make up the classes that describe the motion of a car.

Another kind of motion

Suppose that, as well as being interested in the performance of cars, you have problems to solve in the field of ballistics. You might be a rocket engineer, for example, or a champion rifle shot. You need to be able to calculate the force required to accelerate a spacecraft of given mass. Fortunately, it is an easy calculation:

$$\text{force} = \text{mass} \times \text{acceleration}$$

where force is in newton, mass is in kilogram and acceleration is in metre per second per second. You might also need to calculate the amount of energy needed to accelerate the spacecraft to a given velocity. This is its kinetic energy, given by:

$$\text{K.E.} = \frac{1}{2} \times \text{mass} \times \text{velocity}^2$$

We could write a program similar to *motion* (pp. 27-8), or perhaps split it into more manageable pieces as we did with the *vehicleMotion* class and its associated classes. At this point we begin to realise another advantage of OOP. There is no need to write a completely new program for spacecraft, because a large part of it has already been written for cars. We already have routines for typing in much of the data required, such as initial velocity, acceleration and time. We already have methods for calculating final speed from these. All we need is a routine for typing in the mass of the spacecraft and methods for calculating the force and K.E. We simply need to re-use the existing objects and create a few new ones to use with them.

This is how we set about it:

1) We can re-use the whole of the *motionInput* class as it stands. It declares three essential variables and the methods for keying them in.

2) The *workItOut* class declares two variables and the methods for calculating them. We need to calculate both these variables, so we will retain this class.

3) However, *workItOut* does not go far enough with the calculations. We need to process the equations for force and K.E, shown on p. 87. So we need to declare two more variables and two methods. Also the mass of the rocket enters into the calculations, so the variable `mass` must be declared and keyed in.

All of these operations are catered for by extending *workItOut*. Here is the listing:

```
import javax.swing.*;

class ballistics extends workItOut {

        float mass = 0;
        float force = 0;
        float kineticEnergy = 0;

        public void keyInMass()
        {
                String        value        =        JOption-
Pane.showInputDialog("Mass? (kg)");
                mass = Float.parseFloat(value);
        }

        public void workOutForce()
        {
                force = mass * accel;
                kineticEnergy = mass * finalSpeed * final-
Speed * 0.5F;
}}
```

The listing begins by importing *swing*, ready for keying in `mass`. The class begins by declaring the variables used in the methods which follow. Next is the keying-in method which has the same structure as in *workItOut*, but a different variable and text message.

Finally, the `workOutForce()` method calculates force and K.E. Note the last term in the expression for K.E. It is a **literal** (that is, the number '0.5' its actual numeric value, not a variable name). On reading this, and noticing the decimal point, the computer might take it to be a `double`. This would result in a type mismatch with the other variables which are `floats`. To make it clear that '0.5' is intended to be a `float`, we append 'F' to the value.

4) The rocket input and calculations are spread across three objects, *motionInput*, *workItOut*, and *ballistics*. So far there have been four methods but no `main` method. We write a special class to provide the `main` method that ties together everything in the three other methods. Here it is, the class *rocketMotion*. It corresponds with *vehicleMotion* in the previous set of objects:

```
class rocketMotion {

public static void main(String[] args) {

        ballistics aquila = new ballistics();

        aquila.keyInData();
        aquila.keyInMass();

        aquila.workOutSpeed();
        aquila.workOutForce();

        System.out.println("\nForce = " + aquila.force + "
N\nK.E. = " + aquila.kineticEnergy + " J");

}}
```

It begins by creating a new instance of *ballistics*, called *aquila*. This is named after the constellation of the *Eagle*. It calls the method `keyInData()`, located in *motionInput*. Then it calls `keyIn-Mass()`, located in *ballistics*.

Having obtained the values of all the keyed-in variables, it proceeds to evaluate the values that it has to display. This is done by calling `workOutSpeed()`, located in *workItOut* and `workOutForce()`, located in *ballistics*.

It ends by displaying the values of `force` and `kineticEnergy` on the command screen.

Four classes are active when processing rocket flight data. These and their relationships are illustrated in Fig. 22 overleaf. The classes for car motion are included in the diagram although *vehicleMotion* and *car* are not being used for rockets. As in Fig. 21, overlapping circles indicate a class and one of its instances.

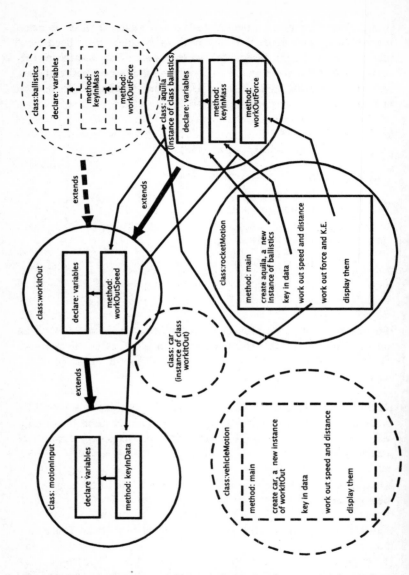

Fig. 22. The objects in use when operating on the motion of a rocket.

Figs. 21 and 22 are attempts to show the working relationships that exist between the members of a set of OOP objects. Some members of the set, such as *motionInput,* perform basic tasks. They can be used in a wide variety of programs dealing with motion — referring to cars, rockets, flying foxes, snooker balls, and much more. The `workItOut` and *ballistics* classes come in the same category, though *ballistics* is a little more specialised because it deals with energy-related aspects of motion. At the other extreme are the most specialised of the classes, such as *vehicleMotion* and *rocketMotion*, which perform special tasks in their `main` method and call on the more general classes to help it to perform them.

Breaking a program into small simple classes gives great flexibility to the programmer, and to others who may want to use some of the more basic classes and methods.

These 'motion' classes are just an illustration of what is an essential aspect of OOP. From the very first program in this book we have called on classes and methods performing limited and usually basic tasks, and written by other people. Frequently-used examples are `System.out.println()`, `Integer.parseInt()` and *String*. This is what OOP is all about.

Things to do

1 Add another category of OOP to the 'motion' programs. For example, to find the distance travelled by a railway train which accelerates from rest for a given number of minutes, then coasts along at constant speed for an equal number of minutes.

2 Write an OOP based on *Divide* (p. 23) or *nutsAndBolts* (p.58). Input should use `JOptionPane` (p. 71). Each program should be broken down into at least three classes.

9 Using constructors

To explain constructors, we need to re-examine what is meant by a class. When we write a class we are creating a model (or plan, or template) for an object that will perform prescribed tasks. Writing a class has similarities to drawing a plan for building a house. The plan specifies what rooms the house is to have, their dimensions and the materials and techniques to be used for building.

The architect's plan is a bundle of papers covered with drawings — it is *not* the house. Similarly, a class is *not* an object, but tells the computer about the object or objects that belong to that class.

As we have already seen on p. 3, a class must have **data**, and **methods** for working on the data. Otherwise, the class can do nothing. A third item of a class is a **constructor**. A constructor is a special kind of method that tells the computer how to build the class. It is not essential to have one, but using a constuctor makes sure that the class is built up exactly as required. This is particularly important if new instances of the class are to be created.

Here is an example that uses a constructor to produce a catalogue of flowers:

```
class flowerCat {

        String flowerColour = "";
        int plantHeight = 0;

        // This is the constructor.

public flowerCat(String colour, int height){
        flowerColour = colour;
        plantHeight = height;

}}

public class flowerData {
        public static void main(String[] args) {

        flowerCat crocus = new flowerCat("yellow", 12);
        flowerCat geranium  = new flowerCat("red", 30);
```

93

```
System.out.println("The crocus has " + crocus
.flowerColour + " flowers and is " + crocus.plantHeight +
" cm high.");
        System.out.println("The geranium has " + geranium
.flowerColour + " flowers and is " + geranium.plantHeight
+ " cm high.");

}}
```

The listing on pp. 93-4 comprises two class definitions. We could have saved them separately, but it is simpler to save them as a single file under the filename *flowerData.java*. This is the name of the *second* class, the one that contains the `main` method.

The two classes are compiled in a single operation by typing *javac flowerData.java*. We do not use the name *flowerCat* when compiling, but *javac* takes note that there are two files and compiles *flowerCat* as a separate .class file.

The program is run by typing *java flowerData*. Although we are not asking the computer directly to run *flowerCat*, the `main` class of *flowerData* instructs it to create two instances of *flowerCat*. So it looks in the *flowerCat* class file to find out what to do. In this way, the computer is told where to find all the required information.

The `flowerCat` class establishes the form of the instance classes that are to be created by `flowerData`. It uses a constructor to do this. Before defining the constructor it declares the two variables to be used to describe each kind of plant. There would probably be more than two variables in practice, but two is enough to demonstrate how a constructor works.

The definition of the constructor begins with this line:

```
public flowerCat(String colour, int height)
```

The constructor has the same name (*flowerCat ()*) as the class that includes it. This is an essential feature of a constructor. It is also an easy way to pick out a constructor when reading a listing. If the name is different, it is probably a class *method*, not a constructor.

94

Another feature of a constructor is that it does not return any values. In contrast, methods can and often do return values and the keyword `return` is used when doing so. The action of `return` is discussed on pp. 99 and 116.

If a constructor takes variable values as parameters, these are listed in brackets following the constructor name. Each is listed as a variable type followed by an identifier. In this example, the identifiers indicate to which feature of the plant the variable refers (colour and height). This makes it easier to read and understand the listing. However there is no need to to this. Instead, the identifiers could be `data0`, `data1`, `data2` and so on.

Following the constructor name with its list of variable types and names by which to identify them, we type a list of the actual names to be used when processing the class instances. For example, each value for `flowerColour` will be a string and will be listed as the first parameter.

If the constructor has no arguments, its name is followed by empty brackets ().

Constructors can do more than just set up lists of variables. We have already used several constructors in our programs without describing them as such. An example is the `JFrame()` constructor used on p. 73. This takes a single parameter, the text message, and displays it on the screen as a fully constructed message panel in the *Windows XP* format as seen on p. 74. An example of additional features of constructors appears in the next listing, on p. 96.

Another example of a constructor

This next example takes the explanation of constructors a stage further. In this program, we are creating *hotelData* objects that list the important features of different hotels. With six items of information for each hotel, the constructor helps to keep the data-processing systematic.

```
class hotelData {

        // Declare variables first.

        String hotelName;
        int starRating;
        int numberOfRooms;
        boolean swimmingPool;
        double rackRate;
        double specialRate;

        //Then  the constructor.

        hotelData(String  data1,  int  data2,  int  data3,
boolean data4, double data5) {

        // Then allocate variable names to the constructor.

        hotelName = data1;
                starRating = data2;
                numberOfRooms = data3;
                swimmingPool = data4;
                rackRate = data5;
                specialRate = data5 * 0.8;
        }

public static void main(String[] args) {

        hotelData hotel0 = new hotelData("Sea View", 3, 20,
false, 150.50);
        hotelData hotel1 = new hotelData("Plaza", 5, 125,
true, 220.00);
        hotelData hotel2 = new hotelData("Grand", 4, 241,
true, 175.25);

        System.out.println("\nThe " + hotel0.hotelName + "
Hotel has " + hotel0.numberOfRooms + " rooms.");
        System.out.println("It has " + hotel0.starRating +
"-star rating.");

        if (hotel0.swimmingPool == true)
        System.out.println("It  has  a  swimming  pool  for
guests.");

        System.out.println("The  daily  rate  for  a  double
room is $" + hotel0.rackRate + ".");
        System.out.println("There is a special rate of $"
+ hotel0.specialRate + " for seniors.");

}}
```

Save this as *hotelData.java*.

Class *hotelData* begins by declaring the various types of hotel data: the name of the hotel, its star rating, the number of rooms, whether it has a swimming pool or not, the daily rack rate for a double room (in dollars), and the discounted special rate (also in dollars).

Then comes the constructor method. The first thing to notice about this is that it has the same name as the class, which is `hotelData()`.

The opening line of the constructor definition is followed by a list of the various kinds of data item, allocating them to their places in the list of parameters.

Note that there are six data items in the variable list but only five parameters in the constructor. This is because the value of one of the data items, `special rate,` is obtained by multiplying the rack rate by 0.8. In this way, the constructor describes a *method* for calculating the discount and assigning it to a variable. This will be a feature of all the class instances created by using this constructor.

The `main` method of the class begins by creating three class instances, `hotel0`, `hotel1` and `hotel2`. With the format of the data having been set out already by the constructor, creating the instances is very simple. We just call the constructor and use `new` to put the data for each hotel into the new instance. In the instance of `hotel0`, we can see from the parameters that it is the Sea View Hotel, a 3-star hotel with 20 rooms. It does not have a swimming pool. Its rack rate is $150.50, discounted to 80%.

Finally, the class prints out the complete data for the Sea View Hotel. Note the `if ...` statement. If it has a pool, this fact is printed out. On the other hand, if it does not have a pool, nothing is said. Hotels do not like to advertise their deficiencies.

In this example, we print out the data from just one of the instances of the class (Fig. 23 overleaf). In a more practical program, such as might be used by a hotel booking agency, the program would be designed so as to print out a selection of one of more of the instances, according to the requirements of the customer.

If constructors are so important, why have we not mentioned them in Chapters 1 to 8, even though we have created many class instances using new. The reason is that *Java* automatically provides a basic constructor whenever a new class is instantiated.

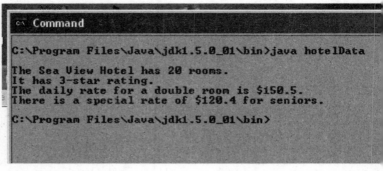

```
C:\Program Files\Java\jdk1.5.0_01\bin>java hotelData

The Sea View Hotel has 20 rooms.
It has 3-star rating.
The daily rate for a double room is $150.5.
There is a special rate of $120.4 for seniors.

C:\Program Files\Java\jdk1.5.0_01\bin>
```

Fig. 23. Details of the Sea View hotel as displayed by hotelData..

Constructors and methods

Constructors have several features in common with methods, so it is easy to confuse them. This is not surprising because constructors *are* methods, though methods of a very special kind. As explained earlier, they are the method for building (or constructing) new class instances. But this is all they do. Any other kind of action, apart from declaring variables, requires a method.

The next listing (pp. 100-101) shows a version of *flowerData* that has had methods added to it and has been generally upgraded. It is called *flowerSpace* and, like *flowerData*, is saved along with the class *flowerCat* which defines the constructor. Class *flowerCat* too has been upgraded and now features three class methods. When new instances of *flowerCat* are created by *flowerSpace* they will all be based on the flowerCat () constructor and include the three methods. So that this version can receive on-screen input, it begins by importing all the *swing* package.

The constructor, `flowerCat()`, comes next after declarations of variables. It is exactly the same as before. It will require two parameters to set up each new class instance, One is the flower colour and the other is the mature plant height. Note that the name of the constructor is the same as the name of the class.

Three class methods follow:

- `flowerIn()` displays a small window on the screen and invites the user to key in the name of a flower. It follows much the same routine as that used in *newInput* on pp. 71-2. The string that is typed in is assigned to the string variable `flowerName`. The method returns this value to the main method by using the line:

        return flowerName;

    This command stops the execution of the method at that point. The computer then returns to processing the main method in *flowerSpace*.

- `showSpace()` is used at the end of the main program to display the output. One of the control words in its definition is `void`, which indicates that the method does not return any values — it simply does a job when called. This is in contrast to `flowerIn()`, which returns a string and has `String` as one of its control words. The form of the `println` statements is very familiar to us by now.

- `apart(int plantHeight)` is a method that calculates the ideal distance apart for the difference species of plant, depending on the value of the argument `plantHeight`. This result of the calculation is assigned to the instance variable `spacing`. The method also tests the size of the spacing. If it is less than 20 cm, a message is displayed suggesting that this species is suitable for use as ground cover. Having been declared at the beginning of *flowerCat*, `spacing` is available to the method and to *flowerSpace*. No return is required, so the method definition includes the word `void`.

The listing of *flowerSpace* is continued on the opposite page.

```java
import javax.swing.*;

class flowerCat {

        String flowerColour = "";
        int plantHeight = 0;
        int spacing = 0;
        int height = 0;

        // This is the constructor.

public flowerCat(String colour, int height){
        flowerColour = colour;
        plantHeight = height;
        }

        // And here are three methods.

        static String flowerIn() {
        String value = JOptionPane.showInputDialog("Flower
name");
        String flowerName = value;
        return flowerName;
        }


        void showSpace(){
        System.out.println("\nThe flowers are " + flower-
Colour);
        System.out.println("They grow to " + plantHeight +
" cm.");
        System.out.println("Spacing is " + spacing + "
cm.");
        }


        void apart(int plantHeight) {
        spacing = 2 * plantHeight;
        if (spacing  < 20)
        System.out.println("\nGood for ground cover.");

}}

public class flowerSpace {

        static String flowerName = "";
```

```
public static void main(String[] args) {

        flowerCat crocus = new flowerCat("yellow", 12);
        flowerCat geranium  = new flowerCat("red", 30);
        flowerCat periwinkle = new flowerCat("purple", 9);

        flowerName = flowerCat.flowerIn();

        if (flowerName.equals("crocus"))
        crocus.apart(crocus.plantHeight);

        else if (flowerName.equals("geranium"))
        geranium.apart(geranium.plantHeight);

        else if (flowerName.equals("periwinkle"))
        periwinkle.apart(periwinkle.plantHeight);

        if (flowerName.equals("crocus"))
        crocus.showSpace();

        else if (flowerName.equals("geranium"))
        geranium.showSpace();

        else if (flowerName.equals("periwinkle"))
        periwinkle.showSpace();

        else
        System.out.println("\nNot listed");
}}
```

The *flowerSpace* class (above) begins by declaring a variable, then goes straight into the main method. This creates three new instances of *flowerCat*, one for each of three species: crocus, geranium and periwinkle. There could, of course, be many more such instances, amounting to a comprehensive catalogue of plants. Three instances suffice to demonstrate the program.

The instances each receive two parameters: the flower colour and the mature height.

Then follows a sequence of operations in which many calls are made to *flowerCat*. The first, to find flowerName, goes directly to the flowerIn() method in *flowerCat*. The string read from the screen is assigned to flowerName. This was defined as a **class variable** at the beginning of the class by using the control word static. It applies to the whole class, not to any particular instance of the class.

The rest of the program consists of a two sequences of if ... else ... routines. In the 'condition' expression, we are matching the typed-in string against a series of plant names that correspond to the instances. Since this is a comparison of strings, we use the equals() method (see pp. 38-9).

The first sequence runs through the instances, calling on the apart() method, and prints out the spacing required for the plant that matches flowerName. If the spacing is small, it also displays the 'ground cover' message. The second sequence runs through the instances, calling on the showSpace() method, and prints out the corresponding flower colours and height.

Finally, if none of the if... else... statements produce a match, the message "Not listed" is displayed. This appears if the user types a name that is not on the list, or makes a spelling mistake.

Fig. 24 shows the program being run.

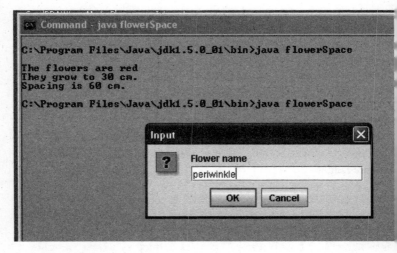

Fig. 24. The flowerSpace *program has been run once already, with 'geranium' as the entry. Now the user is finding information about 'periwinkle'.*

Things to do

1 Write a class and its constructor that handles data about cinema films or TV programmes. Create instances of the class, each holding the data about one film. Data could include the name of the film or programme, names of its main star or TV performer, its category (news, documentary, thriller, sitcom), length in minutes, and (in the case of a film) its audience rating (U, PG, X, etc.).

2 Upgrade the program to allow on-screen input.

3 Add methods that provide such features as the listing of all titles in a given category, or all titles with a given star or performer.

4 Write a class and its constructor, including a few class methods to handle data on any other subject that is your hobby or is of particular interest to you.

10 Errors

We all make mistakes, especially when programming. When something is wrong or goes wrong, *Java* lets us know about it. The program stops running and one or more **errors** or **exceptions** are listed on the screen. Less often we might be given a **warning** that the program is workable but could be improved in some way.

Errors may occur when *javac* is compiling the program or when *java* is running it. In either case the program stops running, the error message appears on the screen, and there is nothing to do but puzzle out where you have gone wrong and correct it.

We will look at several types of error and, in the case of run-time exceptions, consider ways of dealing with them.

Errors when compiling (and after)

This is the type with which you are already well familiar. If you so much as leave out a semicolon at the end of a line, *javac* will complain by sending an error message. Try it by typing in this program *exactly* as printed, and compiling it.

```
class watchIt {

public static void main(String[] args) {

int dividend = 5
int divisor = 2;
int quotient = dividend / (divisor - 2);

System.out.println(quotient);
}}
```

Assuming that you *did* omit the semicolon, and did not make any other mistakes in the typing, the result should be as shown in Fig. 25 overleaf.

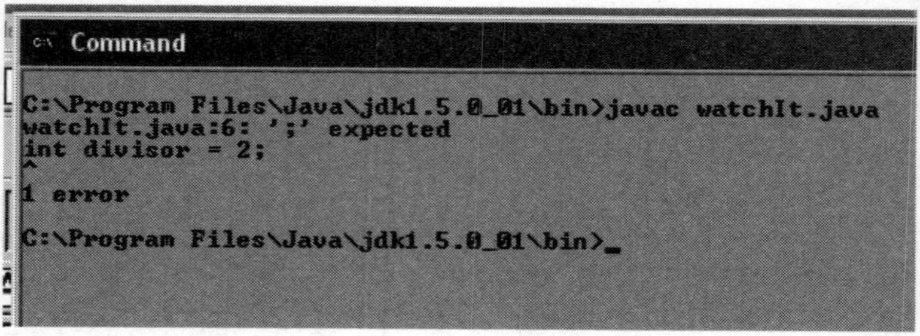

Fig. 25. A very frequent typing error is detected by javac.

The error message says precisely what is wrong. It expected to find a semicolon by the time it reached line 6, but did not find one. Note that *javac* includes blank lines when it is counting program lines. It displays the point in the program at which it detected the omission by printing a ^ under the first character in line 6. This character is not always accurately placed but gives you a clue as to where to start looking for errors.

Reload *watchIt.java* into your text editor and add the missing semicolon at the end of line 5. Save it and use *javac* to compile it. All goes well and compilation is successful.

Now run the .class file, using *java*. Fig. 26 shows what happens.

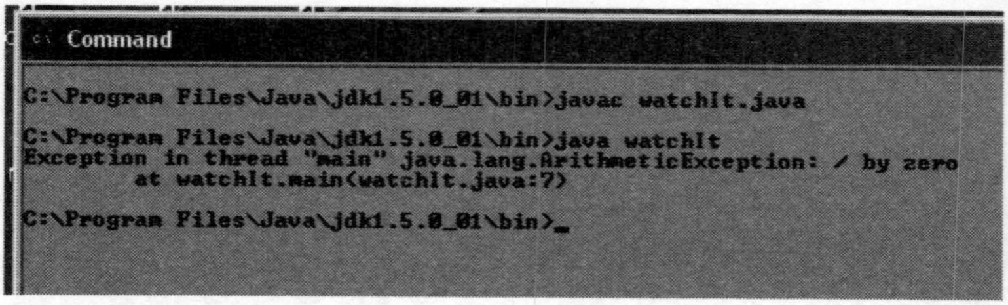

*Fig. 26..*watchIt *compiles correctly with* javac, *but* java *throws an exception at runtime.*

106

Because of deliberately careless programming, we have tried to divide 5 by zero. Mathematically, the result is infinity, but *java* can not cope with such inexpressible large numbers and throws an exception error.

More compile-time errors

We demonstrated the divide-by-zero errors just to emphasis that a program may compile correctly yet fail to run. Now to look at some more of the errors that frequently occur at compile-time. Fig. 27 is an example.

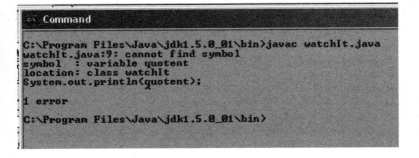

Fig. 27. What is the cause of this error?

This occurred when compiling a slightly incorrect version of *watchIt*. Fortunately, it is easy to spot. The listing reads 'quotent' instead of 'quotient' in line 9. The computer looked back in the program and could not find a reference to anything called 'quotent'.

Java does not allow spelling mistakes or typing errors. It is strictly case-sensitive too. For example, it would throw the same error if the word 'quotient' on line 9 had been typed 'Quotient'.

The place in a program in which a variable is declared makes a difference to the way it runs (or does not run!). Try shifting the position of the declaration of dividend. Incidentally, the division-by-zero error has been eliminated in this version.

107

```
class watchIt {

int dividend = 5;

public static void main(String[] args) {

int divisor = 2;
int quotient = dividend / divisor;

System.out.println(quotent);
}}
```

The declaration of `dividend` has been moved out of the `main` method. The result of this small change is shown in Fig. 28.

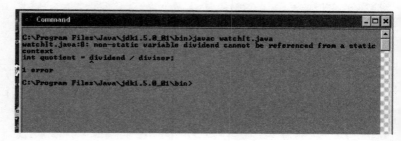

Fig. 28. Another way in which a variable can not be found (or, at least, not be used).

The problem is the `static` statement, which appears in the definition of the method. A method that is declared to be `static` can call only variables that have been declared as `static`. Because `dividend` has been declared as an instance variable (that is, non-static) it can not be used directly in the `main` method. There are two ways of overcoming this problem: move the declaration back into the `main` method, so that it becomes static, or declare it as a static variable:

```
static int dividend = 5;
```

If this change is made, the program compiles and runs without producing error messages.

Warnings

Occasionally, *javac* will issue not an error message, but a warning. Fig. 29 shows an example.

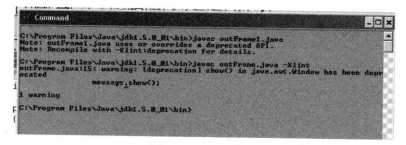

Fig. 29. A warning that the program could be improved.

The figure shows the sequence on the command screen. An attempt was made to compile the class *outFrame1*. This is identical with the listing on p.73, but with the `pack()` method replaced by the `setSize()` method discussed on p. 74. The point at issue is that the final line of this listing is:

```
message.show();
```

When compiling for the first time, *javac* displayed the message:

```
outFrame1.java uses or overrides a deprecated
API.
```

A deprecated API is an older API that has subsequently been replaced with a newer, better one. The message did not state which API was deprecated but invited us to repeat the compilation with a switch that brings up the details. So, as instructed, we typed:

```
javac outFrame1.java -Xlint
```

As shown in Fig. 29, *javac* replied by referring to the last line of the program, saying that the method `show()` has been deprecated.

So far, so good, but we still are not told what method to use instead of `show()`. There was no further help from *javac*, so we turned to the Sun website. The URL is:

```
http://java.sun.com
```

A panel on the left of the home screen is headed 'Reference'. Under this heading, click on 'API Specifications'. In the next main screen there is a 'List of technologies ...'. Click on the first item in this list, J2SE 1.5.0 (assuming that this is the version you are using).

The top of the next screen has a list of options spread across it. Click on 'INDEX'. The top of the next screen has the alphabet spread across it. Click on 'S'. A list of hundreds of APIs appears, with details. Scroll though the list, which is in alphabetical order, until you come to `show()`. This is described as a method in class *java.awt*. It is deprecated as of JDK version 1.1 and replaced by:

```
setVisible(boolean b)
```

Scrolling a few items back in the list brings you to a description of `setVisible()`. It takes a Boolean argument. If b is `true`, the panel is displayed. If b is `false`, the panel is not displayed. The advantage of `setVisible()` over `show()`, is that it can be turned on and off by using `true` or `false`. By contrast, `show()` can only be turned on.

A little experimenting with versions of *bugAlert* (p. 75) showed that the argument of `setVisible()` can be either `true` or `false` as on p. 73, or can be a pair of previously declared Boolean variables with true or false values, or a pair of logic expressions that are true or false. Examples of the latter are $(2 == 2)$ and $(2==1)$

Although *outFrame1* works perfectly well if we ignore the warning and still use `show()`, the on/off feature of `setVisible()` is valuable in programs such as *bugAlert* .

Catching run-time errors

All the errors that have been described above are avoidable by suitable programming, and this is the best way to deal with them. Getting rid of errors means checking the typing and, sometimes, re-writing parts of the program so that errors can not occur. While doing this, your programming skills will inevitably improve, even though your mood may not!

A lot of run-time errors, such as keying in data of the wrong type or in the wrong range, can be predicted. The program can include input routines that reject illegal entries repeatedly until the user supplies a legal one. Careful study of the program can discover if and where a 'division by zero' error might occur and the program can be adapted to take care of this. The same applies to array indexes that are out of range.

Unfortunately, there are some errors that are virtually unpredictable. A file being loaded into the computer is of the wrong length. A program is so complicated with so many alternative routes through it that it is almost impossible to be certain that an arithmetic error will not occur. In cases such as these, *java* will throw an exception. Fortunately, this need not necessarily cause the program to crash.

There are methods in *Java* by which we can **catch** the error. Then we can divert the computer into a routine that deals with the error without making the program crash. These techniques are not described in this book because they are not essential when starting to learn the language.

Summing up Chapters 6 to 10

As well as summing up the five most recent chapters, this section ties up a few loose ends of terminology.

Arrays

Data can be held in the form of an array, which is the equivalent of a list with the entries indexed from 0 upward. The entries must all be of the same variable type and the array is declared using the name of the type:

```
String[] nameOfDay;    or  String nameOfDay[];
double[] pettyCash     or  double pettyCash[];
```

Array length is defined using `new`. String arrays can be defined directly (p. 56).

Casting

Except for Boolean variables, a variable of a given type can be cast into a different type. Use the format:

```
(type)value
```

A type with a smaller range (see p. 60) may be automatically cast into a type with a greater range.

Input and output

Routines from the *swing* package use the system's operating system for the input and output of data. They generate small windows and panes into which data can be typed and from which data can be read. For data input we used the *JOptionPane* class and the `showInput-Dialog()` method (p. 71).

The window has the typical appearance expected in a Windows™ program. It has a header bar, OK and Cancel buttons and, at top right, a Close button.

For output we created an instance of the *JFrame* class, which produces a (usually) small window, containing a message. The frame has a header bar and the usual three 'Minimize', 'Maximise', and 'Close' buttons at the top right corner. To put the window on the screen we use an instance of the *JPanel* class and the methods add(), setContentPane(), pack() and setVisible() (or show()).

The dimensions of the window are controlled by using the pack() method, which makes it just big enough to contain the message, or the setSize () method. The setSize() methods lets us set the dimensions in pixels, including filling the entire screen.

OOP

Chapter 8 discussed the principles of object orientated programming. These are best summarised by Figs. 21 and 22 on pp. 86 and 90.

Constructors

These are special methods for building instances of classes. It is not essential to use them but they help to make the creation of class instances more systematic. A constructor method has the same name as the class that it is to construct.

Errors

Errors due to typing mistakes, spelling mistakes, or forgetfulness are reported when *javac* compiles the program. Compiling stops and can not be re-started until the errors have been discovered and corrected. Other kinds of error include attempts to divide by zero, using array indexes that are out of range, and structuring the program so that the computer can not find the variable. Some of these may not be reported until run-time.

114

Errors and exceptions such as these are best eliminated by carefully checking the programming. In cases where this is difficult or impossible, *Java* provides a way to catch the errors and deal with them.

Variables

Types include primitives and Strings (p. 49-50). Arrays hold several variables of the same type, identified by the index, which runs from 0 upward (p. 55).

Instance variables are declared *outside* a method, preferably listed first within the class definition. *Examples* (from p. 93):

```
String flowerColour = "";
int plantHeight = 0;
```

Note the use of "" to initialise an empty string variable. Instance variables define the attributes of an object. Instance variables are also called object variables because copies of them are created when a new class instance is created. The copies belonging to different objects can take different values.

Local variables are declared *inside* a method, and do not exist outside it. *Example*: loop counting variable j, on p. 42.

Class variables are available to the class as a whole, and have the *same value* for all objects in the class. They are distinguished by the used of the word static when they are declared. *Example* (from p. 100):

```
static String flowerName = "";
```

This is used in all the calls to the different class instances on p. 97.

Constants are prefixed by the word final when they are declared. Their value is declared at that time and can not be changed. *Examples*:

```
final int discount = 20;
static final double ounceToGramme = 28.34952;
```

Use of variables by methods

If a method operates on instance variables (declared outside it) it does not return a value. The word `void` is included in its definition. *Example* (from p. 100): method `showSpace()` uses instance variables `flowerColour` and `plantHeight`, declared at the beginning of class *flowerCat*.

If a method creates a variable inside itself it returns that variable to the `main` method on exit from the method. Example: the method `flowerIn()` on p. 100 creates string variable `flowerName`. The last line of the method is:

```
return flowerName;
```

The return type (in this example, `String`) is specified in the method definition, instead of using the word `void`:

```
static String flowerIn()
```

Note that this method is a **class method**, as indicated by `static`. It is available to any instance of the class (the same as for class variables, opposite). A `static` method can only call other methods that have been declared `static` and can use only `static` variables.

Arguments and parameters

These are found listed in curved brackets `()` after a method name. They have similar functions and it is not too serious a matter to confuse one with the other.

However, a **parameter** is defined mathematically as a value that is constant in any given case but may vary from case to case. This description fits the values that we use when creating class instances, and in many other operations. For example, the quantities `"yellow"` and `12` are constant for the `crocus` object (p. 101). They are different, but constant for the `geranium` and `periwinkle` objects. So they are parameters.

116

An **argument** is a variable that determines the value of a function. An example is `plantHeight`, which determines the value of `spacing` (p. 100). So `height` is a parameter when it is being used to create the plant instances but is an argument when used in the `apart()` method.

Access specifiers

These encapsulate objects so that access to them (the ability to use them, to read variables, to change values and similar abilities) is available to restricted categories of object. There are four levels of access, usually set by a keyword that must always come first in the definition:

1) No specifier (the default level): available to any other objects in the same package. Examples (p. 100):

```
class flowerCat
int plantHeight = 0;
```

2) `public`: available to all classes in a package. The `main` method is always public. Example (p.101):

```
public static void main(String[] args)
```

3) `protected`: access limited to subclasses and other classes in the same package.

4) `private`: access limited to the same class, and not to subclasses of that class.

Classes can be declared only as `public` or with no specifier. This is because it would not be possible to run the class without gaining access to it from some other class. Methods and variables can be granted any of the four levels of access.

The last two specifiers described above are of more use when building up complex programs.

Final modifier

As well as being used to declare a variable that takes a constant value (see p. 115), final can also be used to modify classes or methods.

A final class can not be used to make a subclass. A final method can not be overridden by a method of the same name in a subclass.

In the prevous paragraph, the term 'overridden' refers to the situation in which a method defined in a subclass has the same name as one in the class above it (the superclass). If the method in the subclass is called in the subclass, *java* executes the subclass method and ignores the class method. Making the class method final prevents this.

11 *Java* packages

A **package** is a group of related classes. The packages are grouped together into a larger group called *java*.

Examples of packages include:

- **java.lang**, which contains all the fundamental classes needed to implement the *Java* language. It is essential for running any *Java* program. It is loaded automatically when a program is run. Examples of java.lang classes include: Float, Math, and Void.

- **java.util**, provides many utility classes, such as ArrayList, Calendar and Random.

- **java.awt**, contains the classes of the abstract windowing toolkit. The classes deal with many kinds of user interface, such as buttons, sliders, and pull-down menus.

- **java.io** contains classes concerned with input and output of streams of data through hardware such as keyboards, printers and modems.

A more recent package, *javax.swing*, covers much the same ground as *java.awt* but with a wider range of functions and with more powerful classes. We used classes from this package in Chapter 7 to produce input and output windows on the screen.

Grouping the classes and methods into packages has advantages. The number of resources in *Java* increases year by year. It becomes difficult to find new names for new classes, without resorting to long and sometimes obscure titles. If they are grouped into packages, each item in a package can only call or be called by a member of the same package. There is no package-to-package accessibility. This means that different classes or methods in different packages operate without the risk of confusion or the risk of one interfering with the other.

When you write a new class, this does not automatically become a member of a named package. New classes belong to a default package that has no name. However, it is possible to create a new package and place any of your newly-developed classes in it.

Classes from `java.lang`

Success in *Java* programming relies heavily on being familiar with what classes and methods are available in these and other packages. The full list is available on the Sun website (p. 110) and lists of the generally useful classes and methods are given in the more advanced *Java* manuals. To get you started, this book describes in detail a few interesting objects from each package. Items from the *swing* package are explained in Chapters 13 and 15.

`currentTimeMillis()`

This first example of a *java.lang* method returns the time in milliseconds that has elapsed since 1st January 1970. As you might expect, such a long number requires a long integer to hold it. Also, as you might expect, the function is only as accurate as the setting of the real-time clock in your computer.

The milliseconds elapsed since 1970 is rarely of interest. More often, we want to know the time elapsed since some more recent instant in the past. In this simple use of the method to create a stop-watch we record the initial time when the program is run, with the final time when you click on a button. The difference is your reaction time. Here is the listing:

```
import javax.swing.*;

class reactionTime {

public static void main(String[] args) {

long initial;
long current;
long reaction;
```

```
initial = System.currentTimeMillis();

JOptionPane.showInputDialog("Press OK");

current = System.currentTimeMillis();

reaction = current - initial;

System.out.println("\nYour reaction time is " + reaction +
" ms.");

}}
```

The timed period (initial) begins as soon as showInputDialog is called. This is only *called*, it is not used to return a keyed-in string.

There are many possible uses for this method. Several are discussed in the 'Things to do' section at the end of this chapter.

Mathematical methods

The Math class is a large and important one in the *java.lang* package. We have already used two of its methods: round() in *convertTemp* (pp. 36-8) and random() in *Limerick* (pp. 62-4).

There are methods for calculating sine, cosine, tangent, arcsine, arccosine and arctangent. These have the general form:

double name-of-function(double arg)

The name of the function is the same as the conventional mathematical name, for example:

```
double tangentOfAngle = tan(1.6);
```

The argument is in radians. For those who prefer to work in degrees, there is a method toDegrees() and the reverse method toRadians(). Both operate on double values.

Another useful method for arctangents is double atan2(double *x*, double *y*), which returns the angle which has a tangent *x/y*.

The *Math* class also has some comparator functions, such as max()
which, given two different values, returns the larger one. Here it is
used in a very simple program:

```
class findBiggest {
public static void main(String[] args){;
int values[] = {3, 9, -2, 12, 5};
for (int j = 0; j < 4; j = j + 1) {
        values[j + 1] = Math.max(values[j], values[j + 1]);

        }
System.out.println("Maximum is " + values[4]);
}}
```

The program runs through the values in the array from left to right,
taking them a pair at a time. In each pair it picks out the bigger and
stores this in the right-hand location of the pair. When it reaches the
right-hand end, the maximum value is in the rightmost location of the
array. To see how this works, try a 'dry run' on a piece of paper.

The max() method also works with longs, floats, and doubles
returning the maximum in the corresponding type.

The final example of a *Math* method calculates square roots. Here is a
quick demonstration of its action:

```
class sqRoot {
public static void main(String[] args) {
        double number = 0;
        double root = 0;
        double fiveRoot = 0;

        if (args.length > 0) {
        number = Double.parseDouble(args[0]);

        root = Math.sqrt(number);
```

```
System.out.println("\nThe square root of " + number + " is
" + root);
        fiveRoot = 5 * root;
        System.out.println("Five  times  that  is  " + five-
Root);
}}}
```

The program calculates and displays the square root of a value typed
on the command line. We have added two more lines at the end of the
program to multiply the result by five and display it. Why we did this
will be apparent in a moment.

When we ran this class we aimed to trick it by putting in a negative
number. Square roots of negative quantities are impossible, though
mathematicians and electronics engineers have developed ways of
working with so-called 'imaginary numbers'. Does *Java* have an
imagination? It did not throw an exception, but see what happens in
Fig. 30. Moreover, having found that the result is 'not a number', then
five times that result is 'not a number' either.

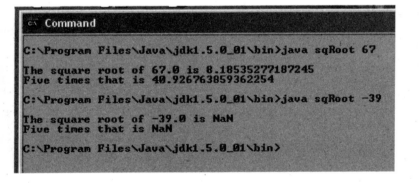

*Fig. 30. Two runs of the square root method. The first shows it
finding the square root of 67 with double precision. In the second run, it is asked to find the square root of –39. It tries, but
decides that the result is 'not a number'.*

123

The *java.util* package

Many of the classes in this package are concerned with processing lists of data, for that is an operation that is often required in database applications. A specialised example of a class from this package is *StringTokenizer*, which we used in *FlightLegs* (pp. 17-19).

A utility method that is simple to use is found in the *date* class. Here is how to use it:

```
import java.util.*;

class showTodaysDate {

public static void main(String[] args) {

Date today = new Date();

System.out.println(today);

}}
```

This displays the day of the week, the month, the day of the month, the time (hours, minutes, seconds), the time zone, and the year. This is comprehensive, and there are a number of methods for setting the time and comparing times, but it is not possible to separate out the various items relating to data and time. There is a more powerful class called *Calendar,* which allows greater flexibility. This program shows it producing just an abbreviated date:

```
import java.util.*;

class shortDate {

public static void main(String[] args) {

Calendar date = Calendar.getInstance();

System.out.print("The date is " + date.get(Calendar.DATE)
+ " / "
+ (date.get(Calendar.MONTH) + 1) + ".");

}}
```

124

The program creates a new instance of Calendar. This new object has many methods built in to it, including the current month, day of month, and the time. All that remains to be done is to print out text, calling:

```
date.get(Calendar.DATE)
date.get(Calendar.MONTH)
```

Note that the months are indexed from 0 to 11, so it is necessary to add 1 before displaying it.

Things to do

1 The *reactionTime* program can also be used for timing longer intervals, such as lap times in a race. Modify the program to make it display the elapsed time in seconds to the nearest hundredth of a second, or to the nearest second, or to the nearest minute.

2 Adapt the *reactionTime* program as a short-interval timer. For example, it could be turned into an egg-timer, running for 5 minutes and then displaying an "Egg cooked" message on the screen. There are many possible variations on this theme.

3 Adapt the *findBiggest* program to accept values typed on the command line. Try to program it to accept any number of values.

4 Adapt the *findBiggest* program to accept values typed in at the keyboard and then find their maximum.

5 There is also a *Math* method called min(), which returns the minimum of two values. Use this method to find the minimum of a set of numbers.

6 Extend the program of problem 5 to find both the maximum and minimum of a set of numbers, then calculate and display the range. Remember that, as the program scans through the array, it alters many of the original values.

7 Write a program that makes use of the *Date* class.

8 Write a program using the *Calendar* class to display the present time. Methods that you might use are `Calendar.HOUR`, `Calendar.MINUTE` and `Calendar.SECOND`. There is also `Calendar.YEAR`. The date can be reset to another date by using methods such as `date.set(Calendar.MONTH)`.

12 More about *swing*

Our previous encounter with *swing* was in Chapter 7 where we used it to provide a more familiar look to input and output routines. Our programs looked more like typical *Windows* programs. From now on we shall use *swing* classes and methods to give our programs a more polished user interface. We will add variety by displaying a range of colours, fonts and graphics.

The visual appeal of *swing* is based on the use of standard pre-programmed **components**. These include the devices so often seen on a *Windows* screen — buttons, sliders, labels, areas for entering text, and drop-down lists. Having got together the components, we need something to put them in, a **container**. Containers include frames, which are windows with a title bar and with buttons to maximise, minimise and close the window. They may have a menu bar and a scroll bar as well. Figs. 18 and 19 on p. 74 show a typical window generated by using the *JFrame* class. Containers may be simpler than this, such as the message pane in Fig. 17, p. 72.

```
import javax.swing.*;

public class selectIt extends JFrame {

        JButton coffee = new JButton("Coffee");
        JButton tea = new JButton("Tea");
        JButton chocolate = new JButton("Chocolate");
        JButton soup = new JButton("Soup");

        public selectIt() {
                super("Hot drinks!");
                setSize(300, 100);

        setDefaultCloseOperation(JFrame.EXIT_ON_CLOSE);
                JPanel drinks = new JPanel();
                drinks.add(coffee);
                drinks.add(tea);
                drinks.add(chocolate);
                drinks.add(soup);
                setContentPane(drinks);
                }
        public static void main(String[] args) {
                selectIt drinksVendor = new selectIt();
                drinksVendor.setVisible(true);     }}
```

Fig. 31. An inviting user interface, produced by using JFrame *methods.*

This program has some methods in common with the *outFrame* program on p. 73 but this one invites the user to make some input by pressing one of the buttons.

Since Chapter 7 we have covered more aspects of the *Java* language so we can look at this program with better understanding. It begins by importing the *swing* package. This will be necessary for almost all the programs in Chapters 13 and 15. Next, we declare that the new class *selectIt* extends the *JFrame* class. This means that this new class has access to all the many methods included in the *JFrame* class.

To begin the class definition, we declare the **components** that are to go into the new window. These are four JButton() objects. Each has an identifier (coffee, tea, chocolate and soup) and each is created as an instance of the JButton() object of the *selectIt* class. The text to appear on each button is given as a String argument.

Now we start to put the *selectIt* class together into a **container.** We construct it, using a constructor to do so. The constructor has the same name, selectIt, as the class. It does the following things:

- Calls the super() method to place text on the title bar of the frame.
- Calls the setSize() method to set the width and depth of the frame in pixels.
- Calls the setDefaultCloseOperation() method to set what happens when the user clicks on the 'Close' button (×).

- Creates `drinks`, a new instance of `JPanel`. This is the simplest of the containers, but has a very useful range of features.
- The next four lines place the components (the buttons) in the container. This is done one at a time by calling the `add()` method.
- Calls the `setContentPane()` method, to set the content of the `drinks` panel.

This completes the constructor of the *selectIt* class. Next comes the definition of the `main` method, which creates *drinksVendor*, a new instance of the class and calls `setVisible()` to display it on the screen.

The panel can be dragged to any part of the screen in the usual way. It can be minimised and maximised by clicking on the appropriate buttons in the title bar. Its shape can be changed by dragging its edges. Note that the buttons are not fixed in position. If there is enough width they arrange themselves in a single row across the top of the panel. If the panel is narrow, they appear in a single vertical column, nicely centred.

The typical changes of appearance of a button are already programmed in. A button changes its appearance as the mouse moves over it, and the image changes to a 'pressed button' image when you click on it. Nothing happens because the program has no output routine at present.

Adding icons

The purpose of a button is often clearer if it carries an icon instead of a text label. On p. 130 is an example in which one of three functions in a program is selected by clicking on a button. The images were taken from the author's CD-ROM, *Newnes Interactive Electronic Circuits*. They are 50 pixels square and saved as .gif files. To run this program you will need three icon files saved in the same directory as *Java*. This is usually the '*bin*' subdirectory of the '*jdk1.5.0_01*' directory. There are collections of icons available on CD-ROM or on the web.

The listing is as follows:

```
import javax.swing.*;

public class selFunction extends JFrame {

        ImageIcon scope = new ImageIcon("butt1.gif");
        JButton osc = new JButton(scope);
        ImageIcon animate = new ImageIcon("anibutt.gif");
        JButton anm = new JButton(animate);
        ImageIcon problem = new ImageIcon("butt2.gif");
        JButton prob = new JButton(problem);

        public selFunction() {
                super("Select a function");
                setSize(350, 100);

        setDefaultCloseOperation(JFrame.EXIT_ON_CLOSE);
                JPanel funcs = new JPanel();
                funcs.add(osc);
                funcs.add(anm);
                funcs.add(prob);

                setContentPane(funcs);
                }
        public static void main(String[] args) {
                selFunction NIECfuncs = new selFunction();
                NIECfuncs.setVisible(true);

}}
```

This program has the same sequence of actions as *selectIt*, but has only three buttons. These select three possible ways of studying a given circuit: analyse it electronically, show an animated diagram of its action, solve problems concerning it. The only additions in this program are the three lines in which the three .gif images are made into ImageIcon objects. The button objects are then given the value of an ImageIcon.

Fig. 32. Icons provide a user-friendly way of labelling buttons.

130

Events

Before going on to explore the full range of components and containers, we will investigate ways of making something happen when the user clicks on a button. In the terminology of event handling, the button is known as a **source**. Clicking on a button or changing the state of other sources such as check boxes and sliders, generates an **event**. An **action event** occurs when a button is pressed, or a menu item is clicked on or an item on a list is selected. There are special methods, known as **listeners**, which are there to detect such events and act accordingly.

The *selFunc* program is based on these principles. The input side of it is similar to *selFunction*.

```
import javax.swing.*;
import java.awt.event.*;
import java.awt.*;

public class selFunc extends JFrame implements ActionListener {

        ImageIcon scope = new ImageIcon("butt1.gif");
        JButton osc = new JButton(scope);
        ImageIcon animate = new ImageIcon("anibutt.gif");
        JButton anm = new JButton(animate);
        ImageIcon problem = new ImageIcon("butt2.gif");
        JButton prob = new JButton(problem);
        String message;

        public selFunc() {
                super("Select a function");
                setSize(350, 100);

        setDefaultCloseOperation(JFrame.EXIT_ON_CLOSE);
                osc.addActionListener(this);
                anm.addActionListener(this);
                prob.addActionListener(this);
                JPanel funcs = new JPanel();
                funcs.add(osc);
                funcs.add(anm);
                funcs.add(prob);

                setContentPane(funcs);
                }
```

```
public static void main(String[] args) {
            selFunc NIECfuncs = new selFunc();
            NIECfuncs.setVisible(true);
}

public void actionPerformed(ActionEvent button) {
            Object source = button.getSource();
            if (source == osc)
                    message = "Analyse circuit";
            if (source == anm)
                    message = "Animated diagram";
            if (source == prob)
                    message = "Solve problems";

            System.out.println(message);
}}
```

This program has very basic output, which we shall improve upon shortly. For the moment, we are content to detect (or listen for) an action and make some kind of response. The response of *selFunc* is simply to display text in the command window.

Running through the program from the start, we find the following points:

- It begins by importing the *java.awt.event* and *java.awt* packages. The letters '*awt*' are short for **Abstract Windowing Toolkit** (p. 119). These packages were the forerunners of *swing*. Although *swing* classes have largely superseded the equivalent *AWT* classes, we still need to use *AWT* for event handling.
- Note the additional words in the line in which the class is defined. The clause implements *ActionListener*, which is an **interface**. Its purpose is to link an event to an action. When an action event occurs, the interface calls on its method, actionPerformed() to carry out the action. More detail on interfaces is outside the scope of this book.
- The declarations have an extra line, declaring message.
- The definition of the constructor contains three lines adding the three sources (the three buttons) to the *ActionListener*. This ensures that clicking on these buttons will be detected. The argument is this, referring to the current object, the button.

132

- `actionPerformed()` is the method of the *ActionListener* interface. Its argument is an `ActionEvent` object, which we have named `button` in this program.
- The problem with *ActionListener* is that it detects when an event has occurred but does not directly indicate which component was the source of the action. This can be determined by using `getSource()` to return the name of the source which caused the event. An object is declared, named `source`, which holds a String that is the name of the source.
- Three `if...` statements then deal with the identity of the source and what to do about it. Each compares the value of source with the value of the name of one of the buttons.
- The String `message` (declared at the beginning of the program) is then assigned an appropriate message. This is displayed on the command screen.

Note that this program does not simply run from beginning to end and then stop. *ActionListener* remains continuously alert and a message is displayed whenever an event occurs. The program ends only when the user clicks on the 'Close' button at top right.

Modifications

The *selFunc* program would look better if it displayed the frame in the centre of the screen and lower down. This is easy to arrange. Delete this line:

```
setSize(350, 100);
```

Replace it with this line:

```
setBounds(250, 100, 350, 100);
```

Re-compile and re-run the program to see the effect. The arguments used are numbers of pixels and (in order) mean: *x*-position of left edge of frame from left edge of screen, *y*-position of top edge of frame from top of screen, width of frame, height of frame.

So far, we have let *Java* take care of how the buttons are arranged in the frame. If you play around with the size and shape of the frame, using the mouse to drag its borders you will soon see what is happening. The program locates the buttons in order from left to right beginning at the top of the frame. If the line is full, it puts the next buttons on the second row, and so on. Finally, the rows of buttons are centred.

This arrangement of buttons is called the **flow layout**. It is the default layout if you do not specify anything different. We can exercise a little more control by using the `FlowLayout()` method. This requires two extra program lines, which go just after we have created `funcs`, the new instance of `JPanel`:

```
FlowLayout rgt = new FlowLayout(FlowLayout.RIGHT);
funcs.setLayout(rgt);
```

Fig. 33 shows the effect of adding these two lines to the program.

Fig. 33. Flow layout of the buttons aligned at the right end of each line. If the frame is wider, there will be a group of two or three buttons, but the group will be at the right end of the line.

Other arguments that can be used with `FlowLayout()` are `LEFT` and `CENTER` (note the spelling).

Grid layout places the buttons (or other components) into a grid consisting of a specified number of rows and columns. The command is:

```
GridLayout fourByTwo = new GridLayout(4, 2);
funcs setLayout(fourByTwo);
```

You can use any identifier instead of `fourByTwo`. The arguments are the number of rows, and the number of columns. With only three buttons, you might expect this to fill the top row, place the third button in the first column of the seconds row and leave five empty cells. Fig. 34 shows what happens.

Fig. 34. `GridLayout()` *may produce some strange effects (see text).*

It has produced four rows and filled them from top to bottom. The second column does not appear. Perhaps this is because the buttons expand to completely fill all the available space. This differs from flow layout where there is a small gap between columns and rows.

In grid layout, we can specify the size of horizontal and vertical gaps like this:

```
GridLayout twoByFour = new GridLayout(2, 4, 20, 30);
```

To accommodate this neatly, we need to change the dimensions of the frame to 150 pixels square. The result is shown overleaf.

Fig. 35. A frame with gaps between the rows and columns.

Now the rows appear to have been filled as requested — but what has happened to the two unfilled columns? It seems that this method works best when we fill the whole grid. Note that there is no gap between the buttons and the edge of the frame.

Another version

Now we set out to build a program that uses *swing* for both its input and output. The program is called *quiz*. It asks a question and presents buttons labelled with four possible answers. The user clicks on one of the buttons and a comment appears in a frame. First we will get the input side of the program working. It is listed opposite.

The listing has the same structure as *selFunc* (pp. 131-2) but uses different names. First it creates four buttons, named after four cities. One of these is the capital of New Zealand.

Next comes the definition of the constructor, also named *quiz*. The question is in its header bar.

```java
import javax.swing.*;
import java.awt.event.*;
import java.awt.*;

public class quiz extends JFrame implements ActionListener
{

        JButton sydney = new JButton("Sydney");
        JButton wellington = new JButton("Wellington");
        JButton auckland = new JButton("Auckland");
        JButton christchurch = new JBut-
ton("Christchurch");
        String message;

        public quiz() {
                super("Which is the capital of New
Zealand?");

                setSize(450, 100);

        setDefaultCloseOperation(JFrame.EXIT_ON_CLOSE);
                sydney.addActionListener(this);
                wellington.addActionListener(this);
                auckland.addActionListener(this);
                christchurch.addActionListener(this);
                JPanel capitals = new JPanel();
                capitals.add(sydney);
                capitals.add(wellington);
                capitals.add(auckland);
                capitals.add(christchurch);
                setContentPane(capitals);
                }
        public static void main(String[] args) {
                quiz quiz1 = new quiz();
                quiz1.setVisible(true);
}

        public void actionPerformed(ActionEvent button) {
                Object source = button.getSource();
                if (source == sydney)
                        message = "Sydney is in
 Australia!";
                if (source == wellington)
                        message = "Correct";
                if (source == auckland)
                        message = "It is the biggest city
in NZ,\nbut not the capital.";
                if (source == christchurch)
                        message = "A beautiful city, but
not the capital.";

                System.out.println(message);
}}
```

137

We have made the frame a little wider because there are four buttons this time, instead of three. After setting the closing operation, we put the four buttons into contact with the *ActionListener interface*.

To complete construction, we add the buttons to the frame (we are building a panel called `cities`) and set its content.

The `main` method creates an instance of `quiz`, called `quiz1`. It then calls `actionPerformed()` to detect when a button is clicked on and to place the name of the button in the object called `source`.

A sequence of four `if...` statements then identifies the button and sets the string, `message`, to an appropriate response. This is displayed in the command screen in the usual way.

Try typing this in, compile it and run it. The result should look like Fig. 36. One thing to note about this, which you may have already noticed in *selFunc* (p. 131-2) is that the program continues running, *after* you have clicked on a button. You can click other buttons or all four buttons as many times as you like, and the corresponding message is added to the screen. The only way to close the program is to click on the 'Close' button at the top right corner of the frame.

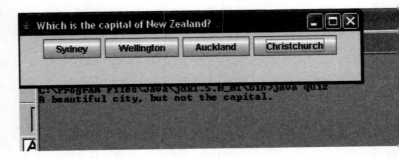

Fig. 36. The result of running the quiz *program, then clicking on the "Christchurch" button.*

138

This point illustrates the difference between a procedural program and an object-orientated program such as this. In a procedural program we would need a loop structure or a GOTO command to return the computer to the beginning of the program to wait for the next click on a button. In this OOP it is like having an intruder detector in a room, waiting for the sound of the 'click'. It is 'switched on' all the time, waiting for an event to occur.

We have let the program run continuously so that the user can explore the answers to the quiz. However, if you want to allow only one attempt at the correct answer, add this line at the end of the program, just before the two closing brackets, }}:

```
System.exit(0);
```

This switches off the listener as soon as one click has been detected, and the program ends.

Swing output too

Load *quiz* into your text editor. An easy improvement is to centre the panel of buttons on the screen. To do this, delete the setSize() method in the constructor and replace it with:

```
setBounds(150, 100, 450, 100);
```

The places it 150 pixels from the left of screen, 100 pixels from the top, and makes it 450 pixels wide and 100 pixels high. Then delete the last line of the program, which puts message on the Command screen and replace it with these lines:

```
JFrame answer = new JFrame();
      answer.setDefaultCloseOperation(JFrame.EXIT_ON_CLO
SE);
      JLabel answerLabel = new JLabel(message);
      JPanel panel = new JPanel();
      answer.setBounds(250, 250, 100, 50);
      panel.add(answerLabel);
      answer.setContentPane(panel);
      answer.pack();
      answer.setVisible(true);
```

This segment of program sets up a frame called `answer`, and sets its 'Close' operation. We also set up a `JLabel` called `answerLabel` to carry the `message` string, and a `JPanel` called `panel` to contain the label.

Next we set the bounds of `answer` so that it comes just below the frame with the buttons. We add the answer label to the panel, and set the content of the panel within the answer frame. Then we pack the frame to hold the message neatly and make it visible. Fig. 37 shows the result.

Fig. 37. The result of running the full version of the quiz program and then clicking on the "Auckland" button.

Things to do

1 Write a class to display four buttons for controlling a washing machine. The buttons are labelled "Hot wash", "Normal wash", "Delicates" and "Start". The buttons are to be arranged in a vertical row.

2 Find suitable icons and substitute these for the washing program names in the class that you wrote for the previous item.

140

3 You can put both text *and* an icon on a button, using this format:

```
JButton (text, icon)
```

The *text* is a string in double quotes (as on p. 127) and the *icon* is the filename of the icon image (as on p. 130). Try this with the classes you have written for items 1 or 2 above. Alternatively, try it with any other programs in this chapter that use JButton.

4 Program the washing machine class to display suitable responses on the command screen when one of the buttons is clicked on (see *selFunc*, p. 131).

5 Write a class with buttons labelled with an unfamiliar word on each button. Clicking on the button displays the meaning of the word on the command screen.

6 Write a program called 'Who is it?'. Set up about 10 buttons each with a photo of a well-known person on it. Before clicking on a button, the user has to guess who it is. When the button is clicked, the name of the person is displayed on the command screen. Or you could write 'What is it?' with problem photos (odd angles, small clips from larger photos) on the buttons.

7 Adapt the complete *quiz* program (pp. 137-9) for other topics and questions.

13 Handy *swing* methods

This chapter consists of a range of methods, briefly described, that you can use to expand and enhance your programs.

Message window

You may wish to flash up a warning message, a helpful hint, or words of explanation on top of the main display of your screen. Or you may want to begin a program with a title or some text that introduces it. For these purposes you can use a JWindow. This is similar to a JFrame but does not have a title bar or the maximise, minimise or close buttons. In other words, the reader can not get rid of the message, but must wait until the window is closed by the program. The *title* class listed below shows how to produce such a window.

```
import javax.swing.*;
import java.awt.*;

public class title extends JWindow {

        JLabel heading = new JLabel("This is the heading");

        public title () {
        super();
        setSize(800, 600);
        JPanel words = new JPanel();
        words.add(heading);

        setContentPane(words);
        }

public static void main(String[] args) {
        title intro = new title();
        intro.setVisible(true);
        for (int j = 0;j < 80000; j = j + 1) {
        for (int k = 0;k < 80000; k = k + 1) { } }
        intro.setVisible(false);

System.exit(0);
}}
```

As listed, this program displays a window taking up the whole screen, and staying there for about 10 seconds. The size of the window and the time for which it is displayed depend on the computer, so some adjustments of values may be necessary. The text is displayed in the centre of the top line.

The program first declares a label called heading, and gives it the value "This is the heading". This is the single component that is to be displayed, though there could be more.

The constructor creates a container called title and sets its size. Then it creates a panel (a sub-container) called words and adds heading to it. Finally, the constructor calls setContentPane to place words inside the outer container, title.

Check Boxes

These are small square components that become checked when they are clicked on. Conversely, when a box is already checked it loses its tick when clicked on. Occasionally boxes are used singly, but more often we set up a panel of checkboxes. The user checks one or more of the boxes to provide information to the program.

In the next program, checkboxes are used by a customer to select from a range of travel brochures.

```
import javax.swing.*;

public class travel extends JFrame {

JCheckBox box1 = new JCheckBox("Britain");
JCheckBox box2 = new JCheckBox("Europe");
JCheckBox box3 = new JCheckBox("Scandinavia");
JCheckBox box4 = new JCheckBox("Russia");
JCheckBox box5 = new JCheckBox("USA & Canada");
JCheckBox box6 = new JCheckBox("India");
JCheckBox box7 = new JCheckBox("Pakistan & Sri Lanka");
JCheckBox box8 = new JCheckBox("Thailand");
```

```
public travel() {
        super("Please tick areas of interest.");
        setBounds(300, 50, 350, 150);
        setDefaultCloseOperation(JFrame.EXIT_ON_CLOSE);
        JPanel areas = new JPanel();
        areas.add(box1);
        areas.add(box2);
        areas.add(box3);
        areas.add(box4);
        areas.add(box5);
        areas.add(box6);
        areas.add(box7);
        areas.add(box8);
        setContentPane(areas);
}
public static void main(String[] args) {
        travel   trvl = new travel();
        trvl.setVisible(true);
}}
```

The program sets up eight checkbox objects, giving each a text label. The constructor adds these to the `areas` panel, one at a time, and the content pane is set. The main method creates a new frame called *trvl* and makes it visible. Fig. 38 shows the result.

Fig. 38. Customers can select one or more brochures by ticking the labelled checkboxes.

The menu could be laid out more clearly by using grid layout (p. 135) but this does not affect the operation of the checkboxes, so we will not add this complication to the demonstration.

145

Radio Buttons

Radio buttons are small circular components reminding one of the buttons on a radio set with press-button tuning. They have an action similar to checkboxes. In the next program a hotel guest selects breakfast from a menu displayed on a console in the hotel room.

```
import javax.swing.*;
import java.awt.*;

public class breakfast extends JFrame {

JRadioButton but1 = new JRadioButton("Fruit juice");
JRadioButton but2 = new JRadioButton("Cornflakes");
JRadioButton but3 = new JRadioButton("Muesli");
JRadioButton but4 = new JRadioButton("Boiled egg");
JRadioButton but5 = new JRadioButton("Scrambled egg");
JRadioButton but6 = new JRadioButton("Fried egg and
bacon");
JRadioButton but7 = new JRadioButton("Tea");
JRadioButton but8 = new JRadioButton("Coffee");

public breakfast() {

        super("Please tick your breakfast choices.");
        setBounds(300, 50, 350, 150);
        setDefaultCloseOperation(JFrame.EXIT_ON_CLOSE);

        JPanel menu = new JPanel();
        menu.add(but1);
        menu.add(but2);
        menu.add(but3);
        menu.add(but4);
        menu.add(but5);
        menu.add(but6);
        menu.add(but7);
        menu.add(but8);
        setContentPane(menu);
}
public static void main(String[] args) {
        breakfast  bkfst = new breakfast();
        bkfst.setVisible(true);
}}
```

The display is shown in Fig. 39, opposite. Using the mouse, the user can select or de-select any item on the menu. Most hotels would not allow this, as a guest could elect to have 'the lot'!

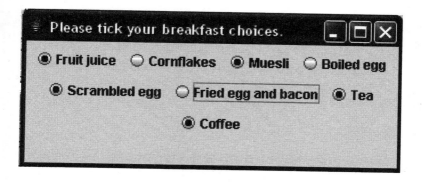

Fig. 39. Radio Buttons are a convenient way of selecting from a menu.

Fortunately, such gourmandising can be prevented by grouping the buttons. This is done by creating **button groups**. For the breakfast we need three groups, for cereal, egg, and beverage. Fruit juice is an option that stands on its own.

This is how to do it. Add these lines to the program immediately after the setDefaultCloseOperation() line:

```
ButtonGroup cereal = new ButtonGroup();
ButtonGroup egg = new ButtonGroup();
ButtonGroup beverage = new ButtonGroup();

cereal.add(but2);
cereal.add(but3);
egg.add(but4);
egg.add(but5);
egg.add(but6);
beverage.add(but7);
beverage.add(but8);
```

First we create three button groups. Then we add the required buttons to each group. Edit the program to include these extra lines. Compile and run the program, then try selecting your favourite breakfast. The display looks exactly the same as before, but now you can select only one item from each group.

There is still the problem that, after you have selected one item of a group, you can cancel it only by selecting another item from the same group. For example, once you have selected one of the egg dishes, you can change it for another egg dish, but you are forced to have an egg dish of some kind. You can not opt out of egg altogether! The solution is to include a 'Cancel' button in each ButtonGroup.

Text Field

This is another kind of component that can be added to a frame. It consists of a box holding a single line of blank screen. There are three ways of calling this:

- JTextField() gives a blank field.
- JTextField(*int*) in which the integer determines the length of the field.
- JTextField(*string, int*) in which the field contains a text message and *int* determines the length.

Fig. 40 shows a text field added to the breakfast menu program.

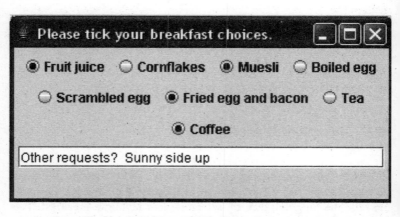

Fig. 40. An editable text field allows the guest to make special requests.

The text field was first displayed with a message in it, asking "Other requests?". In this example the user has typed a reply, referring to her fried eggs: "Sunny side up".

The text field is added to the program by three extra program lines. The first is after the declarations of radio buttons:

```
JTextField request = new JTextField("Other re-
quests?",30);
```

Next, after the list of button groups:

```
request.setEditable(true);
```

This allows the user to type in and edit text. The argument `false` would prevent it. Finally, at the end list of additions to `menu`:

```
menu.add(request);
```

The text field could be placed among the radio buttons by putting this line earlier in the list.

A related component is a **text area**, which is several lines deep. The method for this is `JTextArea()`. The parameters are (*int, int*) or (*String, int, int*), where the integers are the numbers of rows and columns.

If you want the text to wrap round normally at the ends of lines, that is, to carry to the next line *between* words, include these two lines:

```
setLineWrap(true);
setWrapStyleWord(true);
```

Dialog boxes

We have already used one type of dialog box. On p. 71 we described an **Input** dialog box. This asks a question and has a text field in which the user types an answer. We used one again on p. 102.

A message dialog box is simpler. It just displays a message and has an 'OK' button that the user clicks on after reading the message. Fig. 41 shows a typical message dialog box.

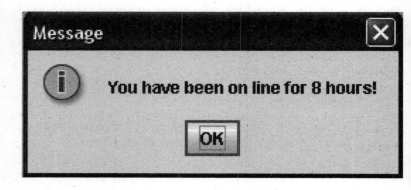

Fig. 41. A message dialog box provides a timely reminder.

This is the program than produced the box:

```
import javax.swing.*;
import java.awt.*;

public class infobox extends JFrame {

        public infobox () {

        setDefaultCloseOperation(JFrame.EXIT_ON_CLOSE);
                JOptionPane.showMessageDialog(null,
 "You have been on line for 8 hours!");
                }

public static void main(String[] args) {
        infobox overtime = new infobox();
        overtime.setVisible(true);

System.exit(0);
}}
```

Responding to input

Most of the programs in this book show a response to input, often by printing a message on the command screen. In this section we are referring to responses which take the form of windows or frames that have a typical *Windows* look. These nearly always involve methods from the *swing* package and often from the *awt* and *awt.event* packages as well.

The *outFrame* (p. 73), *bugAlert* (p. 75), *Birthday* (p. 79) and *motion-Input* (p. 82) programs show how to use the `JPanel()` method to display a message.

There may also be a display when a given event has occurred, such as clicking on a button. For example, the *quiz* program on p. 137 shows that the essential steps in responding to an event are:

- In the constructor, connect each source to the `addAction-Listener()` method, so that it is aware of actions.
- In the `main()` method, set up the `actionPerformed()` method to respond to action events.
- Use the `getSource()` method to find out which source generated the action.

Once the name of the source becomes available, the program can take whatever logical or other action that is required.

The `ActionListener` interface is used in *quiz* to respond to clicking on a button in a panel. It can also be used to respond to clicking on a radio button, a checkbox or a text field. It can therefore be used to respond to input from these components, which have been described earlier in this chapter. On the next page is a listing which demonstrates all four types of response.

To begin with we declare one of each of the four types of component. The frame is set up in the usual way and the four components are added to `ActionListener`. Then they are added to the panel, `comps`.

151

```java
import javax.swing.*;
import java.awt.event.*;
import java.awt.*;

public class eventDemo extends JFrame implements
 ActionListener {

JButton comp1 = new JButton("Press me");
JCheckBox comp2 = new JCheckBox("Tick me");
JRadioButton comp3 = new JRadioButton("Select me");
JTextField comp4 = new JTextField("Keep it brief!", 20);
String message;

public eventDemo () {

        super("Components and events");
        setBounds(250, 50, 300, 150);
        setDefaultCloseOperation(JFrame.EXIT_ON_CLOSE);

        comp1.addActionListener(this);
        comp2.addActionListener(this);
        comp3.addActionListener(this);
        comp4.addActionListener(this);

        JPanel comps = new JPanel();
        comps.add(comp1);
        comps.add(comp2);
        comps.add(comp3);
        comps.add(comp4);
        comp4.setEditable(true);
        setContentPane(comps);
        }
public static void main(String[] args) {

        eventDemo showEm = new eventDemo();
        showEm.setVisible(true);
        }

public void actionPerformed(ActionEvent button) {
        Object source = button.getSource() ;
        if (source == comp1)
                message = "Button";
        if (source == comp2)
                message = "Check Box";
        if (source == comp3)
                message = "Radio button";
        if (source == comp4)
                message = comp4.getText();

        System.out.println(message);

}}
```

152

The text area is given the text message "Keep it brief!" when it is declared and later we make it editable, so that the message can be extended, changed or deleted.

Following the constructor, there is the main method which creates a new frame and then makes it visible. Its appearance is shown in Fig. 42.

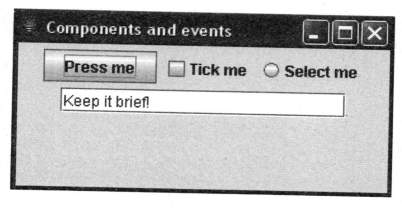

Fig. 42. An assortment of components that demonstrate action events.

To keep the listing as short as possible, the output from the program is sent to the command screen. The last method in the listing shows one way of handling the responses.

The actionPerformed() method detects the source of the action and, using the method getSource(), creates an object holding the name of the source. This is assigned to an object named source.

Depending on the values of source, a sequence of if... statements assign a text string to message.

Finally, the message is printed on the command screen.

There are several other listener methods, responsive to actions on these components and to other happenings. One is the **mouse listener**, which keeps a watch on what is happening to the mouse. For example, it can register **mouse events** such as being clicked on an object, or the keys being pressed or released. Mouse events are particularly useful in Applets.

Key events including pressing or releasing a key on the computer keyboard, are detected by a **key listener**.

Things to do

1 Set up a small 'Welcome' window to show for about 10 seconds and briefly introduce the user to a piece of software.

2 A car insurance compay has a questionnaire for new customers. It lists events that the company needs to know about. "Have you ever been declined insurance?", and "Have you ever been prosecuted for dangerous driving?" are two examples. Build the form using check-boxes. Ask the user to check the box if the answer to a question is "Yes".

3 A hotel asks departing guests to give their opinion on the services provided during their stay. Set up a form with a text area in which the user enters their name, room number, and dates of their visit. Add some radio buttons to rate the various services (Restaurants, Travel bureau, Swimming Pool and so on). For each service there could be a button group including "Good", "Average" and "Poor".

4 Extend the programs you have written for items 3 and 4 to include routines to display on the command screen a summary of the user's responses, using action events.

5 Adapt the program of item 4 to display the output in a Jpanel or a dialog box.

154

14 Applets

The classes that we have built and run in earlier chapters have all been **Java applications**. These are free-standing programs that run under the operating system of your computer. In that respect they are no different from applications written in *C*, *Forth* or *BASIC*.

In this chapter we look at **Java applets**. The distinctive feature of these is that they can be transmitted across the Internet to another computer and run on that computer. It is this feature and the enormous popularity of the WWW that has made *Java* such an important and widely-used programming language.

It might be thought to be a dangerous thing to receive a program that has been sent from another computer. Web users are plagued with viruses sent by malicious persons, devastating their programs and data. But *Java* is not virus-like. There is complete security when downloading an applet from the Internet. The structure of *Java* is such that an applet can not access other parts of the computer and operate on the programs and data stored there.

There are two ways in which you can view applets without putting them on a web site. One is to use your computer's browser, for example, *Internet Explorer* or *Netscape*. It can be used off-line. The other way of viewing employs *Applet Viewer*, a program that is downloaded from Sun as part of the Java Development Kit.

Using Internet Explorer

Before calling up *IE*, we need a file that *IE* can read. This is written in a language called *Hyper-Text Mark-up Language*, or **HTML** for short. The language is fairly simple, being designed mainly for getting your browser to display text and graphics attractively on the screen. We need only a short program to display an applet.

This is the listing of a basic HTML program for displaying an applet:

```
<HTML>
<HEAD>
<TITLE> Demonstrating applets </TITLE>
</HEAD>
<BODY BGCOLOR = LIME>
<H1>Demonstrating Applets<H1>
<P>
<APPLET CODE=message WIDTH=250 HEIGHT=150>
</APPLET>
</BODY>
</HTML>
```

The program has its instructions contained within pairs of **tags.** A tag consists of a keyword enclosed in angle brackets. Examples are <HTML> and <H1>. Opening tags like these tell IE to start doing something. There are also closing tags, which contain a slash, to tell IE to stop doing that thing. Examples are </HTML and </H1>.

An HTML program begins with <HTML> and ends with </HTML>. These tags tell IE that everything between these tags is an HTML program. Within this, the program is in two main sections, the HEAD and the BODY. The HEAD section (typed between <HEAD> and </HEAD> tags) contains general information about the file, but this does not appear on the computer screen. In the listing above, the HEAD contains only the title, between <TITLE> and </TITLE> tags. Unlike a class name in a *Java* program, the title does not have to be the same as the filename.

The BODY section of this program begins with the tag <BODY>, and there is a command in the same tag to make the background colour lime green. We do this so that you can see the extent of the applet, which will have a white background in this example. The first item in the body is the heading that will be displayed on the screen. This is enclosed between <H1> and </H1> which indicates that it is to be displayed in the largest of the standard sizes for headings.

Then comes <P> which begins a new paragraph. This does not have a closing tag.

156

Next within the body is the command to activate an applet. The tag for this includes several directions. 'CODE = message' gives the name of the compiled *Java* class file, 'message.class'. Note that we give only the file name, not the .class extension. The width and height of the applet display area are given in pixels.

Finally, the program is ended with the closing tags </APPLET>, </BODY>, and </HTML>, in that order.

The first stage in viewing the applet is to type in and save the HTML program. Save it with the filename *Applets* in the same folder as your .java and .class files, but with the .html extension.

First applet

Our first applet is a very short one that simply displays a message on the screen. Here is the listing:

```
import java.applet.*;
import java.awt.*;

public class message extends Applet {

public void init() {

this.add(new Label("Java is great!"));
}}
```

The *applet* and *awt* packages are needed to run this program. It is based on the Applet class, extended to display a particular message. The class contains a single method of the Applet class, called init(). To this we add a new label, "Java is great!".

Type in this program and save it under the filename *message.java*. Then compile it.

To view the applet, first run *Internet Explorer*. If you have a different browser, the details of the next stage may be different but the general procedure in the same.

Click on the text in the address window and type in the following address:

file:///C:\Program Files\Java\jdk1.5.0_01\bin\Applets.html

Note that there are *three* slashes after 'file:' and that the remainder of the slashes are backslashes. You may need a slightly different address if you are running an earlier version of *Java* or if your *Java* programs are stored at a different address.

Click on GO, which will cause *IE* to run the applet message program. The screen should look like Fig. 43.

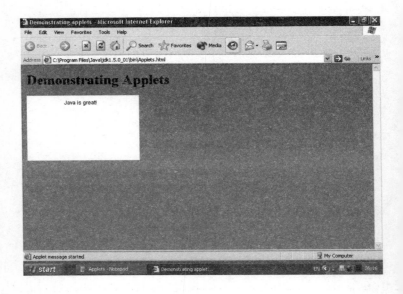

Fig. 43. The computer screen when viewing the message *applet, using* Internet Explorer *off-line. The* IE *area is lime green and the applet is white.*

158

Using the applet viewer

You can use the *Applets* HTML file and the compiled *message* program as before. Call up the command line screen in the usual way. At the prompt, type:

```
AppletViewer applets.html
```

Press Enter and the applet viewer appears at the top left of the screen, as in Fig. 44.

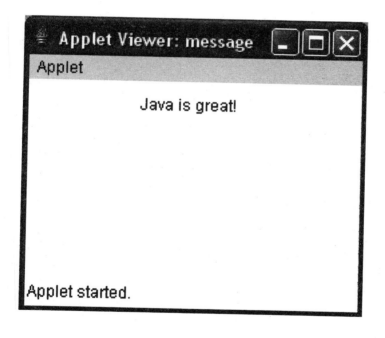

Fig. 44. The applet viewer in action.

The viewer has a drop-down menu (Fig. 45), which is useful for testing the applet.

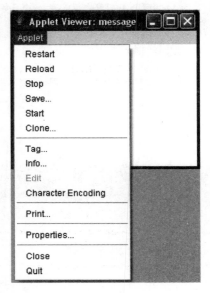

Fig. 45. Clicking on the 'Applet' button at top left produces a drop-down menu.

The functions of the more often-used options are:

- Restart: starts the applet again. Fig. 46 shows what happens.
- Reload: clears the current display and starts the applet again.
- Clone: creates a separate copy of the applet. This can be kept on screen for comparison with later stages of the program.
- Tag: displays the line or lines in the HTML that generates the applet. This is cleared by clicking on the 'Dismiss' button.
- Print: Prints out the applet.
- Close: Closes the copy of the applet in which this option is selected, but not other copies.
- Quit: Closes all copies and the viewer, returning you to the command line.

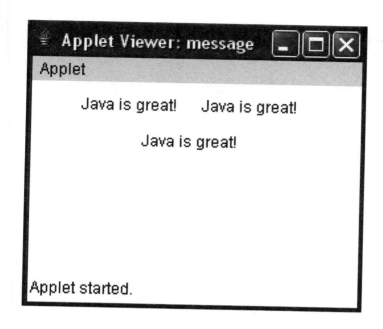

Fig. 46. This is the result of restarting the applet twice.

A simpler way to use the viewer is to place the HTML commands for the Applet in a *comment* in the Java program of the applet. For example, the message program (p. 157) has a comment added to it just before the class definition::

```
import java.applet.*;
import java.awt.*;

/*
<APPLET CODE=message WIDTH=250 HEIGHT=150>
</APPLET>
*/

public class message extends Applet {

public void init() {

this.add(new Label("Java is great!"));
}}
```

Save this as *message.java* and use *javac* to compile it. You do not need the corresponding HTML file. To run the applet, type:

```
AppletViewer message.java
```

The result is the same as in Fig.44.

Applet methods

The very simple applet listed on p. 157 does not illustrate the basic structure of a typical applet program. Applets call on five special methods, which must be called in the correct order. The methods are:

init() Initialises the applet. This is the place for declaring variables. The init() method is called when the applet is first run, but not later in the same session.

start() Always follows after init() and starts the applet running. It is called every time the applet is run, that is every time we run the HTML screen that displays the applet.

paint() This is called to re-draw the applet after it has been partly or wholly overwritten by other display items.

stop() Temporarily stops the applet from running when the browser displays another HTML page. The applet begins running again, from start(), if the user returns to the page.

destroy() The applet is cleared from memory if this method is called after calling stop().

These methods are called automatically when an applet is running. It is not necessary for them to appear in the listing unless there is a particular need to override them. This is why only the init() method is called in *message* (p. 157). The message is added to the initially blank applet. After this, the other methods are called by default. The next applet calls all three of the methods that are used in all but the simplest applets

Coloured text

The *Colours* applet below demonstrates how to produce coloured text on a coloured background. We also use it to illustrate the actions of some of the applets methods listed on p. 162.

Here is the listing:

```
import java.awt.*;
import java.applet.*;

/*
<APPLET CODE="Colours" WIDTH=300 HEIGHT=100>
</APPLET>
*/

public class Colours extends Applet {

        String message;

public void init () {
        setBackground(Color.pink);
        setForeground(Color.blue);
        message = "Blue on pink.";
}
public void start() {
        message += " Started.";
}
public void paint(Graphics g) {
        message += " *";
        g.drawString(message, 10, 50);
}}
```

The listing begins, as always with applets, by importing the *awt* and *applet* packages. A multi-line comment sets up the HTML page.

Before initialising the applet we declare a class variable, which is a string named message.

The init() method is used to set the colours of the background (the screen) and the foreground (the text) to blue and pink, respectively. It also assigns a value, "Blue on pink.", to the variable, message. As we shall see later, this command has no immediate effect on the display. It simply gives message an initial value, stored in memory.

The init() method of an applet must be followed by the start() method. In order to register the fact that the applet is being started, we add the string " Started." to message, so that the value of message becomes "Blue on pink. Started." The program uses the += operator to extend the string.

Now to display the string, using the paint() method. But before we display it, we add a single asterisk to it. The method creates a Graphics object, which we have called g. It could have a different name but g is the one used conventionally.

Key in and save this listing under the filename *Colours.java.* Use *javac* to compile it. Then, at the command prompt, type:

```
AppletViewer Colours.java
```

Press Enter to run the applet. Fig. 47 shows the applet as it first appears. The message appears as blue on a pink background. It has grown to:

Blue on pink. Started. *

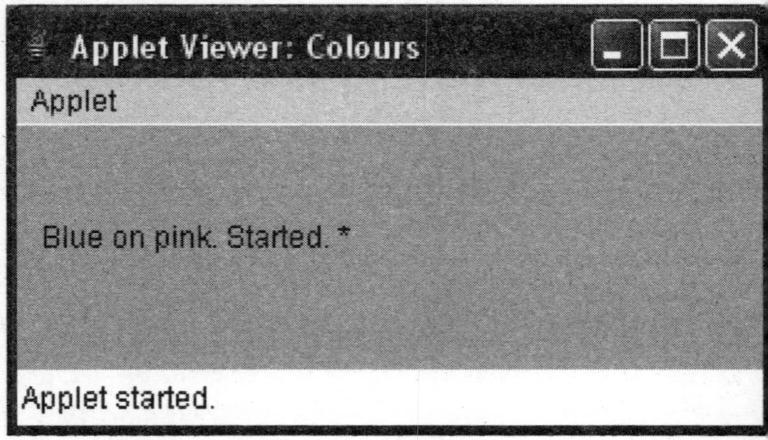

Fig. 47. The Colours *applet when it is first run.*

Without closing the applet down, try playing about with it. For example, drag its right edge to make it wider. Note what happens when you release the left key of the mouse and the background fills in with pink. Alter its shape in other directions.

Now try partly covering it with one of the other windows that are on the screen and then click on the applet to bring it to the front again.

Investigate the effect of minimising the applet by clicking on the left-hand button at its top right. The applet disappears and a button labelled 'Applet Viewer: Colours' appears on the Taskbar. Minimising it leaves it in memory but it is no longer running. Now restore it to its original shape and size by clicking on the button on the Taskbar. What do you notice about the message?

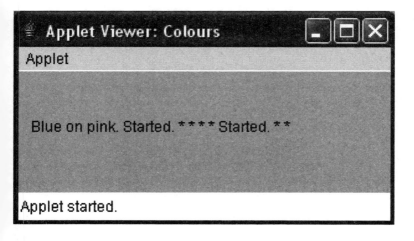

Fig. 48. The Colours applet after it has had to re-paint its display a few times, and has been minimised, then maximised.

Remember that this is a special demonstration of the sequence of applet methods. We would not normally let the appearance of an applet be changed every time it has to re-paint its image.

Try cloning the applet, by clicking on the word 'Applet' on its Toolbar, then selecting 'Clone...' from the drop-down menu. Is the clone identical to the current version of the original?

To show that it is the paint() method that produces the display, reload the original Colours.java textfile and type // at the left end of the line that calls the drawString() method. This converts the line to a comment, which will be ignored by the compiler. Save the new version, compile it and run it. No message appears. Presumably the message is being built up in three stages as before, but it needs the drawString() method to put it on the screen.

Now we will look more closely at drawString(), but before we do this we will get rid of the operations on message. Reload the original textfile and delete (or 'Comment out' with //) the last line of the init() method. Delete the whole of the start() method, which now has no special action to take. In the paint() method, change the += operator to a simple =, as there is now no message to add the asterisk to.

Here is the new version:

```
import java.awt.*;
import java.applet.*;

/*
<APPLET CODE="Colours" WIDTH=300 HEIGHT=100>
</APPLET>
*/

public class Colours extends Applet {

        String message;

public void init () {
        setBackground(Color.pink);
        setForeground(Color.blue);
}
public void paint(Graphics g) {
        message = "*";
        g.drawString(message, 10, 50);

}}
```

When run, this version displays a single blue asterisk on a pink background. It is located half-way down on the left edge of the applet. This demonstrates that there is no need to call the `start()` method if all it has to do is to start the applet in the normal default way.

Incidentally, before or after *Applet Viewer* generates the applet you may see numerous reports of exceptions displayed on the Command screen. These do not seem to affect the running of the applet and may be ignored.

Because of its history, this listing first of all declares `message` as a variable, then gives it a value (*), and finally displays it using the `drawString()` method. However, the displayed string can be defined directly as a literal expression:

```
g.drawString("*", 10, 50);
```

Now is the time to modify the listing in several ways and note the effects. You can change the colours of the foreground and background by altering the colours in the `setBackground()` and `setForeground()` methods. The complete range of colours available is:

black	darkGray	gray	lightGray
pink	red	orange	yellow
green	cyan	blue	magenta
white			

Note the spellings of the greys. The two integer parameters are the coordinates of the beginning of the string.They give the *x*-position and *y*-position, in pixels, with the origin at the *top* left corner of the applet.

Fonts

By default, the text is a 10-point sans-serif style. Other fonts may be employed by using the `Font()` method. There are three parameters: the name of the font, the style (0 = regular, 1 = bold, 2 = italic, 3 = bold italic. The listing overleaf gives examples of font declarations and Fig. 49 shows the results.

Try using other fonts in various sizes and styles. Adjust the size of the applet and the locations of the strings to produce a neat display

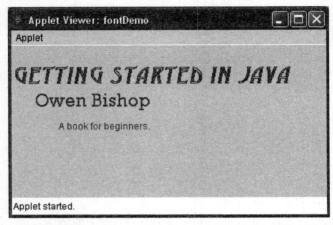

Fig. 49. A selection of fonts in various styles produced by the listing shown below.

```java
import java.awt.*;
import java.applet.*;

/*
<APPLET CODE="fontDemo" WIDTH=400 HEIGHT=200>
</APPLET>
*/

public class fontDemo extends Applet {
        Font title = new Font("Desdemona", 3, 30);
        Font author = new Font("Rockwell",0,24);
        Font blurb = new Font("CourierNew",0,12);

public void init () {
        setBackground(Color.yellow);
        setForeground(Color.red);
}
public void paint(Graphics g) {
        g.setFont(title);
        g.drawString("GETTING STARTED IN JAVA", 0, 50);
        g.setFont(author);
        g.drawString("Owen Bishop", 30, 80);
        g.setFont(blurb);
        g.drawString("A book for beginners.", 60, 110);
}}
```

Drawing lines

The most essential requirement for drawing on the screen is to draw a line. The drawLine() method takes four parameters. The first two of these are the x-distance and y-distance of the beginning of the line. The last two are the x-distance and y-distance of the end of the line.

By default, the line is drawn in black, but it is easy to draw it in any other colour by calling setColor(). This method takes the 'Color' parameters as listed on p. 167 or we can define a new colour, assign it a name and use that, as explained opposite.

```
import java.awt.*;
import java.applet.*;

/*
<APPLET CODE="Lines" WIDTH=400 HEIGHT=250>
</APPLET>
*/

public class Lines extends Applet {
        Color purple = new Color(200,100,200);

public void init() {
        setBackground(Color.yellow);
}

public void paint(Graphics g) {

        g.setColor(Color.red);
        g.drawLine(50, 50, 200, 200);

        g.setColor(Color.blue);
        g.drawLine(50,200,200,50);

        g.setColor(purple);
        for (int x = 100; x < 106; x = x + 1)
              g.drawLine(x, 50, x + 250, 200);

}}
```

The new colour is not one of those listed on p. 167. Therefore we define it as an instance of the Color() object. This takes three parameters that are integers in the range 0 - 255. Respectively, they control the amount of red, green and blue in the colour.

To produce purple, the red, green and blue components are mixed in the ratio 200:100:200. An equal mixture of red and blue produces purple, which is made more interesting by adding a hint of green. Once defined in this way the word *purple* may be used to produce a colour in such methods as setColor().But note that the word is used on its own, as in g.setColor(purple). When one of the 13 standard colours of p. 167 is used, the name is prefaced by color., as in g.setColor(Color.red).

The structure of the program is simple. After declaring the new colour, it sets the background colour to yellow. The paint() method declares three lines, using drawLine(). Each line requires two program lines to produce it. In each case we first use setColor() to set the current drawing colour. Then we use drawLine() to draw the line. This program produces a red line sloping downward from left to right, and an upward-sloping blue line.

The red and blue lines are just one pixel wide, which is rather too narrow for many purposes. There are two main ways of drawing a thicker line. One way is to draw several lines side by side. This is how the purple line is drawn. After setting the drawing colour to purple, we use a for ... loop to draw six lines, each displaced one pixel to the right of the previous line. The result is shown in Fig. 50, opposite.

Applets and Java versions

In this book, the methods used in writing the applets are restricted to *Java 1.0* and *1.1*. This means that they should run on *Internet Explorer, Netscape* and *Applet Viewer*. Most applets were written in these versions until recently because *IE* and other browsers did not support later versions of *Java*. If you have written an applet that does not work properly, it may be that you have used a *Java 2* method. Conversely, when compiling an applet using *javac* you may get warnings about deprecated APIs. Ignore these warnings. The latest *Applet Viewer* should run all versions correctly.

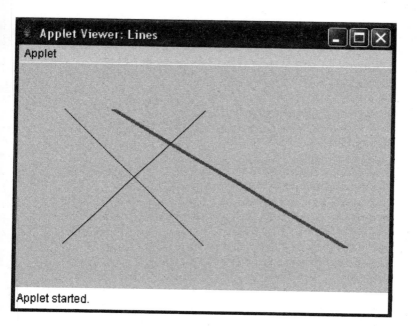

Fig. 50. The result of running the Lines *applet. The purple line on the right is 6 pixels wide.*

The disadvantage of this technique is that the lines have oblique ends. A better approach is to draw a thin rectangle or a thin polygon, as explained later.

Drawing rectangles

Rectangles are drawn by using `drawRect()`. This takes four parameters: the x-position of the top left corner, the y-position of the top left corner, the width and the height. The listing overleaf shows a typical example and Fig. 51 (on p. 173) shows the results. As well as drawing a rectangle of lines, we can fill this in with solid colour by using `fillRect()`. This takes the same parameters.

```
import java.awt.*;
import java.applet.*;

/*
<APPLET CODE="Rectangles" WIDTH=400 HEIGHT=250>
</APPLET>
*/

public class Rectangles extends Applet {
        Color olive = new Color(100, 100, 50);
        Color milkChoc = new Color(200, 150, 50);

public void init() {
        setBackground(olive);
}

public void paint(Graphics g) {

        g.setColor(Color.pink);
        g.drawRect(30, 30, 100, 150);

        g.setColor(Color.green);
        g.drawRoundRect(70, 150, 150, 70, 15, 30);

        g.setColor(milkChoc);
        g.fillRect(100, 50, 240, 40);

        g.setColor(Color.blue);
        g.fillRoundRect(250, 70, 70, 70, 15, 15);

        g.setColor(Color.cyan);
        g.fillRect(150, 190, 220, 5);
}}
```

The program begins by defining two new colours, a medium olive green and a light-brown tone that we have called milkChoc for obvious reasons. It draws an open rectangle in pink. Then it draws one with rounded corners in green. The method, drawRoundRect() takes six parameters. The first four are the same as for drawRect() and the last two set the diameter of the corners in the x and y directions.

The third rectangle is in milkChoc and drawn using fillRect(). The next is a filled rectangle with equal width and height — in other words, a square. Finally we draw a long narrow (5 pixels) filled rectangle in cyan as an example of how to use rectangles to produce thick lines. The main snag of this technique is that the lines must be either horizontal or vertical.

172

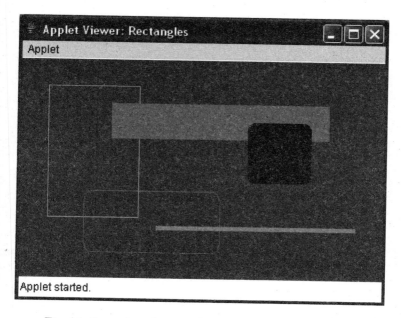

Applet started.

Fig. 51. Examples of rectangles and a line drawn by using
`drawRect()`.

Drawing circles and ellipses

The `drawOval()` method takes four integer parameters that are set by imagining the figure to be enclosed within a rectangular box. The parameters are those that would apply to the box if this were to be drawn.

To illustrate this point, the commands for the first three ovals are simply the commands for the pink, milkChoc and blue rectangles of the previous program but with `drawOval()` and `fillOval()` substituted for `drawRect()` and `fillRect()`. In the case of the rounded rectangles we have omitted the last two parameters as these do not apply to ovals. Fig. 52 shows the ovals. The blue one has equal width and height, so it is a circle. Compare Figs. 51 and 52, to see how the ovals fit within the corresponding rectangles.

```java
import java.awt.*;
import java.applet.*;

/*
<APPLET CODE="Ovals" WIDTH=400 HEIGHT=250>
</APPLET>
*/

public class Ovals extends Applet {
        Color olive = new Color(100, 100, 50);
        Color milkChoc = new Color(200, 150, 50);

public void init() {
        setBackground(olive);
}
public void paint(Graphics g) {

        g.setColor(Color.pink);
        g.drawOval(30, 30, 100, 150);

        g.setColor(Color.green);
        g.drawOval(70, 150, 150, 70);

        g.setColor(milkChoc);
        g.fillOval(100, 50, 240, 40);

        g.setColor(Color.blue);
        g.fillOval(250, 70, 70, 70);
}}
```

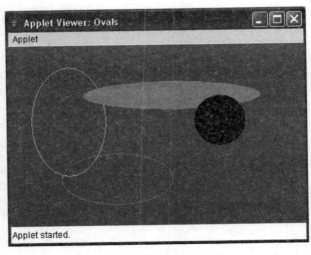

Fig. 52. A selection of ovals.

174

Drawing polygons

The ability to draw polygons is an extremely useful one for creating attractive graphical displays. The polygons have 3 or more sides and the x-distances and y-distances of their vertices are put into two arrays. Then we use drawPolygon() or fillPolygon(), with three parameters: the name of the x-distance array, the name of the y-distance array, and the number of sides. This listing shows two examples.

```
import java.awt.*;
import java.applet.*;

/*
<APPLET CODE="Polygons" WIDTH=420 HEIGHT=480>
</APPLET>
*/

public class Polygons extends Applet {

        Color sky = new Color(150, 200, 255);

public void init() {
        setBackground(sky);
}

public void paint(Graphics g) {

        g.setColor(Color.blue);
        g.fillRect(0, 410, 420, 70);

        g.setColor(Color.white);
        int xDist[] = {180, 180, 340};
        int yDist[] = {60, 380, 380};
        int sides = 3;
        g.fillPolygon(xDist, yDist, sides);

        int xDist1[] = {180, 145, 120, 105, 110, 120, 145,
  175, 160, 145, 140, 150, 160};
        int yDist1[] = {60, 120, 180, 240, 300, 340, 375,
  380, 340, 300, 240, 180, 120};
        int sides1 = 13;
        g.fillPolygon(xDist1, yDist1, sides1);

        g.setColor(Color.red);
        int xDist2[] = {80, 130, 360, 380};
        int yDist2[] = {395, 420, 420, 400};
        int sides2 = 4;
        g.fillPolygon(xDist2, yDist2, sides2);
```

```
        int xDist3[] = {180, 180, 220};
        int yDist3[] = {40, 60, 50};
        int sides3 = 3;
        g.fillPolygon(xDist3, yDist3, sides3);

        g.fillRect(180, 60, 5, 360);

}}
```

Here is the picture, drawn from five filled polygons:

*Fig. 53. Drawing by means of polygons, with
occasional use of other shapes, is an easy way to
produce decorative applets. This one looks really good
in colour.*

The background of the applet is set to a newly-defined light blue
colour, called *sky*. Then a rectangle of darker blue is drawn across the
lower end of the frame to represent the sea.

Next the drawing colour is set to white for the sails, The main sail is a
3-sided polygon, in other words a triangle.

Continuing with white as the drawing colour, the curving jib sail is drawn not with curves but with a series of short straight segments. It is a 13-sided filled polygon.

Finally, the drawing colour is changed to red. The hull of the boat is drawn as a 4-sided polygon. Its opposite sides are not parallel so it is not a rectangle with parallel sides. The burgee is a small red 3-sided polygon, or triangle. The mast is a long narrow rectangle.

This program is an example of **vector graphics**. The image is built up of lines, rectangles, circles and other units. This is the technique employed in the well-known graphics drawing software *CorelDraw!*. The alternative technique is **bit-mapping**, in which the individual pixels of the image are set to the required colours. The highly successful shareware *Paint Shop Pro* is an example of this approach.

With vector graphics, the different items are placed on the drawing area in the order in which they are programmed. Items cover or partly cover other items that are already there. In the *Polygons* applet, for example, the mast covers the left vertical edge of the main sail. It also covers the hull but they are the same colour, so this does not show.

Animations

Animations are widely used in the applets we see on the Internet and many of them are highly sophisticated. Here we demonstrate the simplest possible animation technique which is, nevertheless, very effective. The *Clock* applet displays the image of a clock, with the pendulum swinging vigorously from side to side.

The case of the clock, its dial, and its hands are displayed permanently. Two images of the pendulum, swung to the left and to the right, are displayed alternately. The effect is that the pendulum appears to swing to the left and to the right without it being necessary to display the intermediate stages. This is just one example of the technique, which can be used to enhance applets of many kinds. The listing appears overleaf and is continued on p.179, where there is a screen shot of the display.

```java
import java.awt.*;
import java.applet.*;

/*
<APPLET CODE="Clock" WIDTH=210 HEIGHT=310>
</APPLET>
*/

public class Clock extends Applet {

public void init() {
        setBackground(Color.green);
}

public void paint(Graphics g) {

        g.setColor(Color.darkGray);
        g.fillRoundRect(30, 40, 150, 170, 20, 20);

        g.setColor(Color.white);
        g.fillOval(50, 60, 110, 110);

        g.setColor(Color.blue);
        int xDist2[] = {103, 145, 107};
        int yDist2[] = {110, 145, 110};
        int sides2 = 3;
        g.fillPolygon(xDist2, yDist2, sides2);

        int xDist3[] = {101, 80, 109};
        int yDist3[] = {110, 130, 110};
        int sides3 = 3;
        g.fillPolygon(xDist3, yDist3, sides3);

        while(true){

        g.setColor(Color.orange);
        int xDist[] = {80, 60, 70, 90};
        int yDist[] = {210, 265, 265, 210};
        int sides = 4;
        g.fillPolygon(xDist, yDist, sides);

        g.setColor(Color.red);
        g.fillOval(50, 250, 30, 30);
        for (int j = 0; j < 20000; j = j + 1){
        for (int k = 0; k < 20000; k = k + 1){
        }}

        g.setColor(Color.green);
        g.fillRect(50, 210, 100, 70);
```

178

```
g.setColor(Color.orange);
        int xDist1[] = {110, 130, 140, 120};
        int yDist1[] = {210, 265, 265, 210};
        int sides1 = 4;
        g.fillPolygon(xDist1, yDist1, sides1);

        g.setColor(Color.red);
        g.fillOval(120, 250, 30, 30);
        for (int j = 0; j < 20000; j = j + 1) {
        for (int k = 0; k < 20000; k = k + 1) {
        }}

        g.setColor(Color.green);
        g.fillRect(50, 210, 100, 70);

}}}
```

Fig. 54. The Clock *applet, with the pendulum swinging to the left.*

The applet is initialised with a green background. Then the fixed parts of the image are set down. These comprise four filled figures:

- Case: a dark grey rounded rectangle.
- Dial: a white circle, placed on top of the case.
- Hour and minute hands: two blue 3-sided polygons.

179

The animation takes place within a `while...` loop. This runs for ever, because its argument is true whatever happens.

The animation consists of four repeated stages:

- Display the stem of the pendulum (an orange, 4-sided polygon) and the bob (a red circle) both in the left position.
- Clear the pendulum display by painting a green rectangle over it.
- Display the stem of the pendulum and the bob both in the right position.
- Clear the pendulum display as before.

This technique works well provided that the vectors are small enough to be displayed rapidly.

You may like to see this displayed in Internet Explorer, in which case a suitable HTML file is `Clockhtml.html`:

```
<HTML>
<HEAD>
<TITLE> Demonstrating Clock applet</TITLE>
</HEAD>

<BODY BGCOLOR = LIME>
<H1>The Clock Applet<H1>
<P>
<APPLET CODE=Clock WIDTH=210 HEIGHT=310>
</APPLET>
</BODY>
</HTML>
```

The HTML 'lime' colour is the same as the Applet 'green' colour, so the clock appears on a plain green screen.

Things to do

1 In the HTML program Applets, try altering the text. Add some more text in a smaller font, for example <H3>. Try altering the background colour to maroon, fuchsia, navy, teal or aqua, for example.

2 In the *message* applet, insert different text. Try adding some more labels.

3 Use the *fontDemo* applet as a model for other text displays of your own. Try fonts of different kinds, styles and in different colours. You should be able to call up almost any of the TrueType fonts that are present in your system. To find out what fonts you have, run *Word* and scroll through the list of fonts in the Font Box on the Formatting Toolbar.

4 Drawing rectangles is almost an art-form, as can be seen in Fig. 51. Try some artistic applets yourself.

5 Add white clouds, sea-birds and a dolphin to the sailing picture on p.176.

6 Have fun with lines, rectangles, ovals and polygons. Design an image made up from just one of each of the following: a line, a rectangle, an oval, and a polygon. The figures can be filled or not.

7 Invent some more colours. The three parameters define the amounts of red, green and blue respectively. They must be integers in the range 0 to 255.

8 Try your hand at a two-stage animation, using *Clock* as a model. Possible topics are: children on a see-saw, a Wimbledon spectator whose eyes swing regularly to left and right (make the head turn too?), a clown juggling three clubs, and there are hundreds of other possibilities. You will need a good supply of squared (arithmetic) paper to get the coordinates right.

9 This is strictly for the enthusiast. Extend the technique of *Clock* to build an animation of three, four or more stages.

15 *Graphics2D*

Many methods for drawing graphics have been described in earlier chapters. The methods in Chapter 14, described in the context of applets, can also be used in *Java* applications. However the *Graphics2D* class contains a number of much more advanced methods. In this chapter we present some applications that use a selection of these methods. The methods may be used in applets too but as mentioned on p. 170, some browsers may fail to process them correctly.

An invitation...

Having covered the basics of vector graphics in Chapter 14, the best way to understand *Graphics 2D* is to follow an example. This application, called *invite,* is a party invitation in several colours, using a rectangle, text in two fonts, two ellipses and two lines.

The listing comprises two classes. First we look at the class *invitation*, which defines the graphics elements. It contains several examples of using *Graphics2D* and you will recognise some of the original *Graphics* methods we used for making applets. After this, on p. 186, we will look at the class *invite*, which provides an area to contain the graphics elements and calls *invitation* to put them there.

```
import java.awt.*;
import java.awt.geom.*;
import javax.swing.*;

class invitation extends JPanel {

        public void paintComponent(Graphics g) {

                Graphics2D g2D = (Graphics2D)g;

g2D.setColor(Color.green);
                Rectangle2D.Float background = new
Rectangle2D.Float(0F, 0F, 300F, 200F);
                g2D.fill(background);
```

```
                g2D.setColor(Color.red);
                Font f1 = new Font("Mistral",
Font.PLAIN,28);
                g2D.setFont(f1);
                String greeting = "We're having a party!";
                g2D.drawString(greeting, 50, 40);

                g2D.setColor(Color.yellow);
                Font f2 = new Font("Playbill",
Font.PLAIN,36);
                g2D.setFont(f2);
                String seeYou = "See you there!!";
                g2D.drawString(seeYou, 35, 110);

                g2D.setColor(Color.blue);
                Ellipse2D.Float balloon1 = new
 Ellipse2D.Float(200F, 60F, 50F, 60F);
                g2D.fill(balloon1);

                g2D.setColor(Color.pink);
                Ellipse2D.Float balloon2 = new
 Ellipse2D.Float(230F, 70F, 50F, 60F);
                g2D.fill(balloon2);

                g2D.setColor(Color.white);
                g2D.drawLine(225, 120, 250, 160);
                g2D.drawLine(255, 130, 250, 160);
}}
```

The listing begins by importing the *java.awt* classes and *javax.swing*.
It also imports the geometric package from *java.awt* which is needed
for plotting rectangles, ellipses and other figures.

The whole of the drawing instructions are within the paintCompo-
nent() method. This has a Graphics object, g, as its argument
but this is cast into a Graphics2D object, g2D, by the line:

```
Graphics2D g2D = (Graphics2D)g
```

The g2D object is referenced for the whole of the class definition. The
class defines six graphics elements, in the order in which they are to be
painted. For some of these, the order does not matter. Where there are
overlaps, the element that is to be covered or partly covered is defined
before the element that it is to cover.

Fig. 55. The invitation.

The six elements are:

- **Rectangle2D** This is laid down first to cover the whole area of the frame, to act as a background. The current paint colour for g2D objects is set by calling setColor(). It is set to green. Then comes the definition of the rectangle. The parameter are the same four as described on p. 171 for the drawRect() and fillRect() methods. The difference is that they are float values, not int. If the values happen to be integers, as in this example, follow each with F to ensure that *Java* recognises them to be float. Whereas in Graphics methods we have fillRect() to produce a filled figure, with Graphics2D we use Rectangle2D to obtain the outline, which optionally may be filled by using the fill() method, as here.

Incidentally, there is also a `Rectangle2D.double()` method, in which the parameters are expressed as `double` values.

- **drawString** This has the same parameters as on p. 167. In this example, we set the current paint colour to red. We define a font called `f1` to *Mistral* type-face, regular style and 28-point size. Then we set the current display font to `f1`. We declare a string named `greeting`. Finally we use `drawString()` to place it in the frame. A second set of instructions creates a string named `seeYou` and puts it lower down in the frame.

- **Ellipse2D** This has the same action as `drawOval()`, p. 174, but the 2D method is correctly named, as both methods draw ellipses, not ovals. The parameters are the same except that they are expressed in `float`, not `int`. `Ellipse2D()` uses `fill()` to produce a filled ellipse. In this example, we draw two ellipses, the first is blue. The second is pink and overlaps the blue one.

- **drawLine()** The strings of the balloons are two white lines drawn as *Graphics* objects.

The *invite* class provides the pane in which the graphics are displayed.

```java
import java.awt.*;
import javax.swing.*;

public class invite extends JFrame {

        public invite() {
                super("An invitation...");
                setSize(300, 200);

        setDefaultCloseOperation(JFrame.EXIT_ON_CLOSE);
                invitation demo = new invitation();
                Container items = getContentPane();
                items.add(demo);
                setVisible(true);
        }
        public static void main(String[] args) {
                invite frame = new invite();
}}
```

186

The *invite* class creates a frame of specified size, with text in the title bar and the graphics items of the *invitation* class contained within it. The class has a main() method which calls the frame into existence on the screen.

You can use this class as a model for displaying other frames of graphics items. Simply amend the title message (super) and the dimensions, and replace invitation twice with the class name of your graphics file.

Filling an outline

We have already used the fill() method to fill a rectangle and ellipses with blocks of solid colour. This facility is available in both *Graphics* and *Graphics2D*. But *Graphics2D* has more exciting filling techniques to offer. One of these is the **gradient fill.** This is a shading effect that lets the colour shift gradually between one part of an image and another part. As usual, this is best explained by a demonstration. Fig. 56 shows three examples of gradient filling, though the effect is much less apparent in a black-and-white reproduction. You need to see it in full colour on the screen to appreciate the possibilities of the effect.

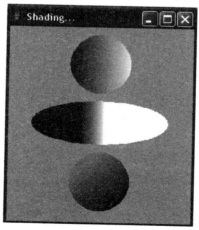

Fig. 56. Three examples of gradient fill, or shading.

187

The background is light grey. The top ellipse (a circle) is shaded from red on the left to white on the right. It has an almost 3D effect, looking like a red sphere illuminated very strongly from the right. In fact, the shading is not quite accurate, but the effect is realistic. In this example the gradient starts (as pure red) on the circumference of the circle at the extreme left. It finishes (as pure white) on the extreme right.

The second example is an elongated ellipse with the start and stop points on the long axis and close together. This makes the ends pure red and pure white with a narrow transition region about half-way.

The third example is another filled circle, with shading ranging from cyan at top left to dark grey at bottom right. The effect is that of a cyan sphere illuminated from the top left, but not so stongly illuminated as in the first example.

The listing of the file *ShadingDD.java*, which produced these examples is as follows:

```
import java.awt.*;
import java.awt.geom.*;
import javax.swing.*;

class ShadingDD extends JPanel {

        public void paintComponent(Graphics g) {

                Graphics2D g2D = (Graphics2D)g;

// The background

                g2D.setColor(Color.lightGray);
                Rectangle2D.Float background = new
Rectangle2D.Float(0, 0, 250, 280);
                g2D.fill(background);

// Top ellipse

                GradientPaint shade1 = new
GradientPaint(80F, 50F,
 Color.red, 160F, 50F, Color.white);
                g2D.setPaint(shade1);
                Ellipse2D.Float topEllipse = new
 Ellipse2D.Float(80, 10, 80, 80);
                g2D.fill(topEllipse);
```

```
// Middle ellipse

                GradientPaint shade2 = new
GradientPaint(95F, 160F,
 Color.red, 125F, 160F, Color.white);
                g2D.setPaint(shade2);
                Ellipse2D.Float midEllipse = new
 Ellipse2D.Float(30, 100, 180, 60);
                g2D.fill(midEllipse);

// Bottom ellipse

GradientPaint shade3 = new GradientPaint(100F, 190F,
 Color.cyan, 150F, 240F, Color.darkGray);
                g2D.setPaint(shade3);
                Ellipse2D.Float bottomEllipse = new
 Ellipse2D.Float(80, 170, 80, 80);
                g2D.fill(bottomEllipse);
}}
```

The listing has the same general structure as the *invitation* class on pp.
183-4. It begins by creating the background as a light grey rectangle
that fills the frame.

Then it defines the top ellipse. All three ellipses are defined in four
stages:

- **GradientPaint()** The six parameters are:
  (*x1, y1*, start colour, *x2, y2*, finish colour)
  The coordinates *x1* and *y1* refer to the point at which the colour
  is pure red. Coordinates *x2* and *y2* refer to the pure white point.
  Coordinates are float and must be declared as such, using F;
  otherwise *javac* will take them to be int and throw a compiling error.

- **setPaint()** This sets the current gradient to the values
  declared above.

- **Ellipse2D()** Creates an instance of an ellipse as described
  on p. 186. Note that this method uses float parameters but
  you do not need to declare them as such.

- **fill()** To fill the ellipse with the current gradient colours.

The class *showShading* provides the frame for displaying *ShadingDD*.
It has much in common with *invite* (p. 186):

```
import java.awt.*;
import javax.swing.*;

public class showShading extends JFrame {

        public showShading() {
                super("Shading...");
                setSize(250, 300);

        setDefaultCloseOperation(JFrame.EXIT_ON_CLOSE);
                ShadingDD demo = new ShadingDD();
                Container items = getContentPane();
                items.add(demo);
                setVisible(true);
        }
        public static void main(String[] args) {
                showShading frame = new showShading();
}}
```

New lines in lines

This rather long listing is a sampler of many of the styles of line made
possible by *Graphics2D*. It is called *LinesDD*, and the class that
displays it is *showLines*. Here is *LinesDD*:

```
import java.awt.*;
import java.awt.geom.*;
import javax.swing.*;

class LinesDD extends JPanel {

        public void paintComponent(Graphics g) {

                Graphics2D g2D = (Graphics2D)g;

// The background

                g2D.setColor(Color.yellow);
                Rectangle2D.Float background = new
 Rectangle2D.Float(0, 0, 300, 350);
                g2D.fill(background);
```

```
// Setting the width of a line

                g2D.setColor(Color.red);
                g2D.draw(new  Line2D.Float(20,   20,   110,
80));

                Stroke widerLine = new BasicStroke(5);
                g2D.setStroke(widerLine);
                g2D.draw(new  Line2D.Float(20,   50,   110,
50));

                Stroke widestLine = new BasicStroke(10);
                g2D.setStroke(widestLine);
                g2D.draw(new  Line2D.Float(20,   80,   110,
20));

// Setting the shape of the end of a line

                g2D.setColor(Color.green);
                Stroke  buttCapLine  =  new  BasicStroke(8,
BasicStroke.CAP_BUTT,
BasicStroke.JOIN_BEVEL);
                g2D.setStroke(buttCapLine);
                g2D.draw(new  Line2D.Float(160,   20,   270,
20));

                Stroke roundCapLine = new BasicStroke(8,
BasicStroke.CAP_ROUND,
BasicStroke.JOIN_MITER);
                g2D.setStroke(roundCapLine);
                g2D.draw(new Line2D.Float(160, 50, 270,
50));

                Stroke squareCapLine = new BasicStroke(8,
BasicStroke.CAP_SQUARE,
BasicStroke.JOIN_ROUND);
                g2D.setStroke(squareCapLine);
                g2D.draw(new Line2D.Float(160, 80, 270,
80));

// Setting the shape of a join between lines

                g2D.setColor(Color.cyan);

                GeneralPath shape;

                g2D.setStroke(buttCapLine);
                shape = new GeneralPath();
                shape.moveTo(10, 120);
                shape.lineTo(80, 180);
                shape.lineTo(10, 180);

                g2D.draw(shape);
```

```
g2D.setStroke(roundCapLine);
            shape = new GeneralPath();
            shape.moveTo(100, 120);
            shape.lineTo(180, 180);
            shape.lineTo(100, 180);

            g2D.draw(shape);

            g2D.setStroke(squareCapLine);
            shape = new GeneralPath();
            shape.moveTo(200, 120);
            shape.lineTo(270, 180);
            shape.lineTo(200, 180);

            g2D.draw(shape);

// Drawing dashed lines

            g2D.setColor(Color.magenta);

            Stroke evenDash = new BasicStroke(5, Basic-
Stroke.CAP_BUTT,
                    BasicStroke.JOIN_BEVEL, 0, new
float[] {10},
                    0);
            g2D.setStroke(evenDash);
            g2D.draw(new Line2D.Float(20, 210, 100,
270));

            Stroke longDash = new BasicStroke(5, Basic-
Stroke.CAP_BUTT,
                    BasicStroke.JOIN_BEVEL, 0, new
float[] {12,4},
                    0);
            g2D.setStroke(longDash);
            g2D.draw(new Line2D.Float(20, 270, 230,
210));

            Stroke dashDot = new BasicStroke(10, Basic-
Stroke.CAP_BUTT,
                    BasicStroke.JOIN_BEVEL, 0, new
float[] {20, 10, 10, 10},
                    0);
            g2D.setStroke(dashDot);
            g2D.draw(new Line2D.Float(130, 270, 270,
210));
```

```
Stroke receding = new BasicStroke(3, BasicStroke.CAP_BUTT,
                        BasicStroke.JOIN_BEVEL, 0, new
    float[]
                {32, 29, 26, 23, 20, 17, 14, 11, 8, 5},0);
                g2D.setStroke(receding);
                g2D.draw(new Line2D.Float(100, 210, 270,
    270));

}}
```

This is the listing of showLines:

```
import java.awt.*;
import javax.swing.*;

public class showLines extends JFrame {

        public showLines() {
                super("Lines...");
                setSize(300, 350);

        setDefaultCloseOperation(JFrame.EXIT_ON_CLOSE);
                LinesDD demo = new LinesDD();
                Container items = getContentPane();
                items.add(demo);
                setVisible(true);
        }
        public static void main(String[] args) {
                showLines frame = new showLines();
}}
```

Type in both *LinesDD.java* and *showLines.java,* compile them, then run *showLines.*

LinesDD produces a panel with five groups of lines, differently coloured. The first group (red) shows lines of different widths. The first is one pixel wide and could have been drawn using draw-Line(), as on p. 169. Here we use a 2D method called draw() which enables a variety of lines to be drawn.

The coordinates of the ends of the line (x1, y1, x2, y2) are expressed in float, but there is no need in this method to append the F to integer values. If we want to define features in addition to width, we do this in three stages:

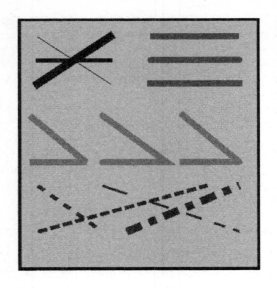

Fig. 57. A sampler of line styles, produced by
LinesDD.

- **setColor()** sets the current drawing colour, in this case, red.

- **BasicStroke()** with a single parameter to indicate the required width, in pixels. We create a new instance of Basic-Stroke(), called widerLine().

- **setStroke()** sets the drawing stroke as defined by Basic-Stroke().

- **draw()** draws a straight line that joins the points indicated by the two pairs of coordinates, and according to the current colour and stroke.

In the sampler we draw widerLine and widestLine, which are 5 and 10 pixels wide, respectively.

Now we move on to consider varying the ends or **caps** of a line (green lines). There are three possible line endings:

- CAP_BUTT, which is the default ending. The line runs from point to point and is cut off squarely at the ends.

- CAP_ROUND, a semicircular cap is added to both ends. Its radius equals half the width of the line.

- CAP_SQUARE, a rectangular cap is added. It is as long as the line width and its width is half the line width. The result of this is to produce a line looking like a CAP_BUTT line but longer by a line's width.

There are three lines in the sampler illustrating these cappings. They are drawn parallel with each other so that we can compare their effective lengths. All three have the same basic length (110 pixels), but those with round and square caps are 118 pixels long (8/2 + 110 + 8/2) when drawn. With a dashed line (see later) the capping is applied to each of its segments.

Programming capped lines follows the same four-stage sequence as above, except that *two* more parameters are required. The first has this format:

```
BasicStroke.CAP_BUTT
```

or one of the other two 'CAP' variables. The second parameter is one of the three 'JOIN' variables. We look at these next. It does not matter which one you choose because it has no effect when we are drawing individual unjoined lines, even though two lines may have their ends at the same point. But you get a compile-time error message if you use just the 'CAP' variable.

The third group in the sample (cyan lines) illustrates three ways of joining lines. However, it is not enough to plot two individual lines originating at the same point and expecting to join them. The lines must be drawn by using the GeneralPath() method. This is explained in the next section but here we just look at the joins.

When we defined the strokes for capping above, we also gave each of these three strokes a different type of join. This has saved a little typing and we can use the same strokes (buttCapLine, round-CapLine and squareCapLine) to illustrate the three joining effects (JOIN_BEVEL, JOIN_MITER and JOIN_ROUND, respectively).

The different types of join are shown in the sampler, from left to right:

- **JOIN_BEVEL**: the bevelled edge cuts straight across from the outer corner of one line to the outer corner of the other.

- **JOIN_MITER**: the outer edges of the lines are continued until they meet.

- **JOIN_ROUND**: the outer edges are smoothly connected by a curved edge.

The sequence for drawing a line with GeneralPath is as follows:

- **setColor()**: sets the drawing color, as usual.

- **declare** a GeneralPath object, called shape in this example.

- **setStroke()**: the stroke has already been defined earlier. Or a new type of stroke can be defined at this stage, and then set.

- **create an instance** of a new GeneralPath and call it shape.

- **moveTo()** specifies the starting point of the path.

- **lineTo()** takes us to the other end of the first segment of the path. Repeat lineTo() for each successive segment.

- **draw()** the path joined as specified by setStroke().

A problem with the mitre join is that with a very acute angle between segments the mitre extends as a long spike. This can be reduced by appending an extra optional parameter when using `Basic-Stroke()`. This substitutes a bevel join if the mitre exceeds a given number of pixels. A suitable value is 10F. We did not limit the mitre in this sampler, mainly to demonstrate the mitre join clearly.

The final group of lines (magenta) in the sampler comprises various dashed lines. These are obtained simply by adding two more parameters to the `BasicStroke()` definition. This brings the total number of parameters to six:

> width
> cap type
> join type (use JOIN_BEVEL by default)
> mitre limit (use 0 if there are no mitre joins)
> new float[] (an array to hold the pattern of dashes)
> dash phase (set the starting point in the pattern)

`new float[]` directly defines a floating point array as on p. 56. Examples are:

- **new float[] {10}** produces a line in which the dashes are 10 pixels long, with 10-pixel gaps between them. See the first line (evenDash) in the sampler. Similarly for other single-value arrays.

- **new float[] {12, 4}** produces a line with 12-pixel dashes and 4-pixel gaps. See the second line (longDash) in the sampler. Similarly for other two-value arrays.

- **a sequence of values** is used to produce a more complex pattern, alternate values referring to dashes and gaps. The pattern is repeated to the end of the line. See the third line (dashDot) and fourth line (receding) in the sampler.

Dash-phase, if 0, starts the line at the beginning of the pattern. If it has a larger value, the line is started that number of pixels into the pattern. We did not use this facility in the sampler.

Drawing 2D polygons and paths

We have already touched on the subject of paths when drawing the angles to demonstrate joining. Drawing a polygon is just a matter of drawing more line segments and connecting the start of the line with the end. We use `moveTo()` to start the path, and `lineTo()` to take it to the next point. This is repeated several times, depending on the number of sides in the polygon. Finally, we use `closePath()` to draw a segment that connects the current position to the beginning of the path.

Polygons are not restricted to regular or slightly irregular figures. The path can cross itself one or more times, giving a variety of complex shapes. It is rather like the traditional game in which one has to draw an object such as a horse or a bicycle with a single line, without lifting the pencil from the paper. Further, the path does not have to be closed (see the sampler). It can have two loose ends to contribute to the artistic effect.

Drawing curved lines

Graphic2D has a range of methods for drawing curved lines. One of the more interesting and useful of these is `curveTo()`, used in the same way as `lineTo()`, which draws straight lines (see above). You may need to play with it for a while to get the line you need. Figs. 58-60 show some examples.

`curveTo()` draws a type of curve known as a Bézier curve. Fig. 58 shows an example. The aim is to draw a curved line from A to B. The line starts off from A in the direction of a control point, control point A. Similarly, the line approaches B from the direction of control point B. When the line is drawn, it runs smoothly from A to B.

To program such a line we use `moveTo()` to get to the beginning of the curve (A). Then we use `curveTo()` with six parameters to define control point A, control point B, and the other end of the line (B), in that order.

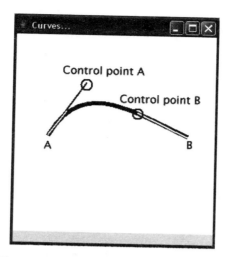

Fig. 58. A simple Bézier curve drawn by the program listed below. The text and construction lines are superimposed on the original display.

Here is the listing for the curve plotted in Fig. 58:

```
import java.awt.*;
import java.awt.geom.*;
import javax.swing.*;

class CurvesDD extends JPanel {

        public void paintComponent(Graphics g) {

                Graphics2D g2D = (Graphics2D)g;

// The background

                g2D.setColor(Color.white);
                Rectangle2D.Float background = new
  Rectangle2D.Float(0, 0, 300, 300);
                g2D.fill(background);

// The curved line

                g2D.setColor(Color.blue);
                Stroke brush = new BasicStroke(6);
                g2D.setStroke(brush);
```

```
GeneralPath squiggle;
                squiggle = new GeneralPath();

                squiggle.moveTo(50, 150);
                squiggle.curveTo(100,  60,  180,  120,  250,
150);

                g2D.draw(squiggle);

}}
```

The line is called `squiggle` and is defined as a `GeneralPath`.
The first move is to (50, 100) whicch is the beginning of the line (A, in
Fig. 58). From the parameters listed for `curveTo`, we can see that
control point A is at (100,60), control point B is at (180, 120), and the
line ends at (250, 150).

This program need a class to call it. The listing for *showCurves.java* is
similar to that of *showLines.java* (p. 193).

By editing and recompiling *CurvesDD.java* it is easy to investigate
where to place the control points to obtain the required shapes. Figs.
59 and 60 show further examples.

*Fig. 59. The effect of moving
control point B to (300, 110).*

*Fig, 60. Control point A is at
(100, 0) and control point B is
at (290, 290).*

In Fig. 59, control point B has been moved to a position above and to the right of B. The result of this is that the line sweeps round to approach B from the 'north-east'. The statement to produce this line is:

```
squiggle.curveTo(100, 60, 300, 110, 250, 150);
```

The control points in Fig. 60 are above and below the direct line from A to B. The statement is:

```
squiggle.curveTo(100, 0, 290, 290, 250, 150);
```

By combining lineTo() and curveTo() several times in the same GeneralPath, there is almost no limit to the variety of outlines that can be produced.

Things to do

1 This chapter has got you started with *Graphics2D*. Now set yourself a few graphics design tasks incorporating text, lines, figures, polygons, and curves. Design windows for inclusion in applets or as stand-alone applications. Possible topics include: a shop sale announcement, a 'We're moving house' notice, a title page for a travel brochure, a 'Thankyou for your gift on my birthday' message, or a snack bar menu.

2 Work out how to draw a dashed, *curved* line, shaped like an 'S', made up of short dashes with rounded ends.

16 Finding the method

When you are writing a program, you may often want to refer back to the classes and methods described in this book. In this chapter we list those classes and methods, and the number of the page on which they are first listed. Usually there is a discussion of the class or method on a nearby page.

Classes

These are the classes that have been specially written for this book. They are listed below in alphabetical order. A very brief description is given when the name of the class does not clearly indicate what it does, or what aspect of *Java* it is intended to illustrate.

In the list, 'A' indicates a class used in an applet. Most of these can be adapted for use in applications. 'C' indicates that it has a constructor (with the same name).

answer	**139**	As *quiz*, but with output to JPanel.
ballistics	**88**	Extends *workItOut* for use with *rocketMotion*.
Birthday	**79**	Input dialogue and message panel on screen.
breakfast	**146 C**	Use of radio buttons and button groups.
bugAlert	**75**	Flashing on-screen message.
Colours	**163, 166 A**	Coloured text.
convertTemp	**36**	C to F and F to C. Conditional logic.
CurvesDD	**199**	Graphics2D, Bézier curves.
DataRead1	**44**	while... loop.
DataRead2	**46**	do...while... loop.

dayNumber	55	Names the *n*th day of the week.
Divide	23	Instantiation.
eventDemo	152 C	Demonstrates types of user dialogue.
findBiggest	122	
FirstProgram	12	Output to command screen.
FlightLegs	17	Use of *StringTokenizer*.
flowerCat (1st version)	93 C	Declares variables for use in *flowerData*.
flowerCat (2nd version)	100 C	Upgraded version for use with *flowerSpace*.
flowerData	93	Displays data.
flowerSpace	100 C	Displays data, including distance apart.
fontDemo	168 A	
GirlsNames	41	`if..., else if..., else...`
hotelData	96 C	Displays data.
infoBox	150 C	Message dialogue box.
invitation	183	Graphics2D text.
invite	186	Container for *invitation*.
Limerick	63	Composes verse at random.
Lines	169 A	Graphics.
LinesDD	190	Graphics2D.
message	157	Applet program sequence.
motion	27	Mathematical operators. Equations of motion.
motionInput	82	Screen input of values for class *workItOut* (see below).
newInput	71	`showInputDialog()`.

nutsAndBolts	**58**	Calculates costs, using arrays.
outFrame	**73**	Using JFrame.
Ovals	**174 A**	Graphics.
pickOut	**66**	Arrays.binarySearch().
Polygons	**175 A**	Graphics (the sailing boat).
quiz	**137 C**	JButton() with text and using *ActionListener* and actionPerformed().
reactionTime	**120**	Uses currentTime-Millis().
Rectangles	**172 A**	Graphics.
RectangularPrism	**33**	Input from the command line. Surface area and volume. Conditional.
rocketMotion	**89**	Calculates force and K.E. Needs *motionInput*, *workItOut,* and *ballistics*.
selectIt	**127**	Demonstrates JButton().
selFunction	**130 C**	JButton() with images.
selFunc	**131 C**	JButton() with images and using *ActionListener* and actionPerformed().
ShadingDD	**188**	Graphics2D, gradient fill.
shortDate	**124**	
showCurves	**200**	Container for *CurvesDD*.
showLines	**193**	Container for *LinesDD*.
showShading	**190**	Container for *ShadingDD*.
showTodaysDate	**124**	
sorter	**65**	Sorts integers in ascending numerical order. Uses Arrays.toString().

sqRoot	**122**	
testEm	**68**	Testing arrays for equality.
timesTable	**67**	Printing out multidimensional arrays, using `deep-ToString()`.
title	**143 C**	Displays a message for a short time.
travel	**144 C**	Uses checkboxes for selections.
vehicleMotion	**84**	Calculates final speed and distance, given initial speed, acceleration and time. Needs *motionInput* and *workItOut*.
waitForMe	**43**	`for...` delay loop.
waitLonger	**43**	`for...` nested delay loops.
watchIt	**105, 108**	Demonstrating errors.
workItOut	**83**	Operates on values collected by *motionInput* (see this and *vehicleMotion*, above).

Methods (and sources of methods)

Most of the items listed below are methods, a few being constructor methods. Those methods which were specially written for the book are indicated by a 'B'. Those methods that apply only to applets are indicated by 'A'. Also we list a few objects that supply often-used methods.

actionPerformed	**132**	Detects action event.
add	**73**	Adds object to container.
addActionListener	**131**	Adds another listener.
apart	**99 B**	Planting distance.

args.length	34	Number of arguments on Command line.
Arrays.binarySearch	66	Returns position of a given no.
Arrays.deepToString	67	Printing multi-dimensional array.
Arrays.equals	68	Compares two arrays for identical content.
Arrays.sort	65	In ascending numerical order.
Arrays.toString	65	Converts array content to a string.
BasicStroke	191	Parameters for Graphic2D line.
ButtonGroup	147	
calculate	23 B	Returns dividend and remainder.
Calendar.DATE	124	
Calendar.getInstance	124	Reads computer's real-time clock.
Calendar.HOUR	126	
Calendar.MINUTE	126	
Calendar.SECOND	126	
Calendar.YEAR	126	
closePath	198	Join current end of Graphics2D GeneralPath line to start of line.
Color	172	Constructor, creates a colour.
Container	186	An object that can contain components.
currentTimeMillis	120	Time elapsed since 1:1:1970.
curveTo	198	Plot Bézier curve.
Date	124	
date.set	126	
destroy	162 A	Delete from memory.
draw	191	Graphics2D.
drawLine	169	Graphics.
drawOval	174	Graphics, unfilled ellipse.

drawPolygon	175	Graphics, unfilled.
drawRect	172	Graphics, unfilled.
drawRoundRect	172	Graphics, rounded corners.
drawString	163	Graphics text.
Ellipse2D	184	Draw unfilled elllipse.
equals	36	Compares two strings, character by character.
fill	183	Fill Graphics2D figure.
fillOval	174	Draw filled ellipse.
fillPolygon	175	Draw filled polygon.
fillRect	172	Draw filled rectangle.
fillRoundRect	172	Draw filled rectangle, rounded corners.
Float.parseFloat	82	Convert numeric string to `float`.
flowerIn	99 B	Inputs name of flower.
FlowLayout	134	Components arranged in rows filled from left to right, top to bottom.
Font	168	Define named font.
GeneralPath	196	A line consisting of two or more straight or curved segments.
getSource	132	Find name of component causing an action event.
GradientPaint	188	Colour of fill grades from one colour to another.
GridLayout	135	Components arranged in specified number of rows and columns.
ImageIcon	130	Image to be placed on a button.
init	157 A	Initialize an applet.
Integer.parseInt	33	Convert a numeric string to an `int`.

JButton	**127**	
JCheckBox	**144**	
JFrame	**73**	
JLabel	**143**	
JOptionPane.		
showInputDialog	**71**	
JOptionPane.		
showMessageDialog	**150**	
JPanel	**73**	
JRadioButton	**146**	
JTextField	**148**	
keyInData	**82 B**	For *motionInput* .
keyInMass	**88 B**	For *ballistics*.
lineTo	**191**	Draws next straight line of a GeneralPath.
main	**12**	*Java* begins with this method.
Math.max	**122**	Returns maximum value.
Math.random	**64**	
Math.round	**38**	
Math.sqrt	**122**	Returns square root.
moveTo	**191**	The start of a GeneralPath.
nextToken	**17**	The next token to be produced by *StringTokenizer*.
pack	**73**	Fit a frame around components.
paint	**163 A**	Display graphics.
paintComponent	**183**	Display Graphics2D.
Printout	**23 B**	Display text output from *Divide*.
Rectangle2D	**183**	Draw unfilled rectangle.
selectIt	**127 B**	Constructor for setting up 'drinks machine'.

setBackground	**163 A**	Colour of screen in applet.
setBounds	**139**	Size and position of frame.
setColor	**169**	Current drawing colour.
setContentPane	**73**	
setDefaultCloseOperation	**73**	
setEditable	**149**	Allow user to edit displayed text.
setFont	**168**	
setForeground	**163 A**	Drawing colour in applet.
setLayout	**134**	Layout of components.
setLineWrap	**149**	Turn line-wrap on or off.
setPaint	**188**	
setSize	**74**	Dimensions of *JFrame*.
setStroke	**191**	
setVisible	**75**	Make frame visible or invisible.
setWrapStyleWord	**149**	Wraps currrent word or current character.
show	**73**	Make frame visible.
showSpace	**99 B**	Display flower data.
start	**162 A**	Runs an applet.
stop	**162 A**	Stops an applet from running.
Stroke	**191**	For *Graphics2D*.
super	**127**	The *super* method is not described in this book, but we use it to put text into the header bar. Must come first in a constructor.
System.exit	**71**	Return to operating system.
System.out.println	**12**	Display text on command screen.
Trigonometric functions	**121**	Various.
workItOut	**28 B**	Method in the *motion* class.
workOutForce	**88 B**	Method in the *ballistics* class.

Postscript ...

Java comprises very many more classes and methods than those listed above. When you have finished this book, you will be ready for more. Consult other books or the *Sun* website (p. 110) to find more classes and methods, how they work, and how to use them.

INDEX

Classes and methods described in this book are listed and described in Chapter 16. They are not indexed here.

A

Abstract Windowing Toolkit (awt) package, 132
access specifier, 117
action listener, 131
animation, 177-80
API, 75
applet, 1
   methods, 162
   viewer, 159-60
argument, 13-4, 36, 117
array, 55, 58, 113
   multidimensional, 62, 67

B

backslash, 9
Bézier curve, 198-9
bit-mapping, 177
Boolean logic, 50
boolean variable, 60
button, 127
button group, 147
bytecode, 8
byte variable, 60

C

case sensitivity, 15
casting, 60-1, 113
catching errors,111
char variable, 50, 60

check box, 144-5

class, 3, 12, 25, 49
   method, 116
   variable, 30-1, 101, 115
colours of text and screen, 9, 163-7
command line, 5, 33-5
comments, 11, 49
compile time, 8
compiling, 15
component, 127-8, 153
concatenation, 19, 79
constant, 51, 115
constructor, 93-5, 98, 114, 128
container, 127
curved lines, drawing, 198

D

data, 4, 20, 49
deprecated API, 75, 109
dialog box, 149-50
double variable, 28, 49, 60
do ... while... loop, 46-7, 52

E

ellipse, drawing, 173-4, 186
else... , 40-1, 51
encapsulation, 4, 12, 24, 49, 119
equality, 38-9, 69

errors, 8, 16, 43, 48, 105, 114
escape codes, 21, 29, 49
event, 131, 153
exception, 43, 48, 105
extends, 83

F

fill with colour, 171-6, 187
final, 51, 118
float variable, 28, 49, 60, 88
floating point variable, 60
flowchart, 2-3
flow layout, 134
font, 167
for... loop, 42

G

GeneralPath object, 196
gradient fill, 187
graphics objects, 184
grid layout, 135

H

HTML, 155-6

I

icon, 129
identifier, 24, 50
if ... , 39-41, 51
import, 20
inheritance, 84
instance, 4 , 24, 51
    method, 24
    variable, 115
integer (int) variable, 18, 24, 26, 49, 60
input-output (io) package, 119

interface, 132
Internet Explorer, 155-8

J

Java language, 1, 21
java, packages, 119
    program, 8, 16
javac program, 8, 15-6
javax package, 119

K

key listener, 154
keywords, 12

L

language (lang) package, 119
layout, 134-5
lines, drawing, 169-71, 190-6
listener, 131
literal value, 88
local variable, 42, 115
long variable, 60

M

main method, 13, 49, 83
Math class, 38
method, 4, 12, 22, 49, 98-9
modulo operator, 25
mouse listener, 154

O

object, 2
OOP, 1, 2, 49, 81, 86, 90-1, 139
operators, 29, 53
ovals, drawing, 173-4

P

package, 17, 119
parameter, 13, 117
polygons, drawing, 175-7, 198
precedence, 29, 54
primitives, 50, 60, 115
private specifier, 117
procedural programs, 3, 81
protected specifier, 117
public specifier, 13, 117

R

radio button, 146-8
rectangles, drawing, 171, 185
return, 116
rounding, 38
run-time, 8
    errors, 111

S

SDK (Software Development
        Kit), 1
short variable, 60
source (of event), 131
static, 13, 24, 108, 116
string, 14, 17
String class, 50
strings, drawing, 186
StringTokeniser class, 17
swing package, 71
Sun Microsystems, 1
    website 5, 110

T

tag, 156
text field, 148-9
Tiger, 1, 65, 67, 69

token, 17
typing errors, 106-7

U

unicode, 76-8
utilities (util.) package, 17

V

variables, 115
vector graphics, 177
void, 13, 116

W

warning, 75, 105, 109
while ... loop, 44-5, 52
writing a program, 8, 11

Notes